METALLICA
RELOAD

Management: Q Prime Inc.

Transcribed by Jeff Jacobson
Front Cover Artwork by Andres Serrano
Photography by Anton Corbijn

D1210787

 Visit our website at www.cherrylane.com

CONTENTS

To find out what's up in the world of Metallica, check out The Metallica Club, the worldwide fan club that's completely guided, controlled, and overseen by the band. Send a self-addressed stamped envelope to:

The Metallica Club
P.O. Box 18327
Knoxville, TN 37928-2327

(from outside the United States, please include an International Response Coupon)

Or e-mail your full name and address to:

METCLUB@aol.com
Metallica Worldwide Web Address:
www.metclub.com

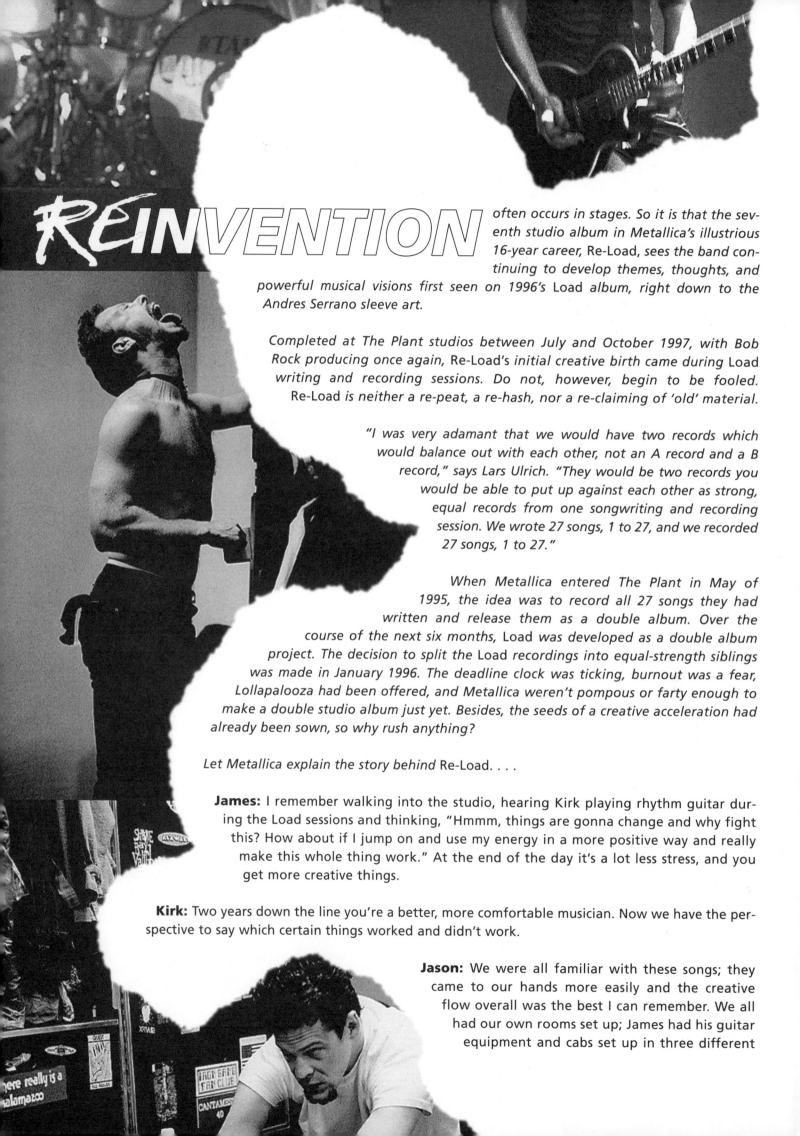

REINVENTION

often occurs in stages. So it is that the seventh studio album in Metallica's illustrious 16-year career, Re-Load, sees the band continuing to develop themes, thoughts, and powerful musical visions first seen on 1996's Load album, right down to the Andres Serrano sleeve art.

Completed at The Plant studios between July and October 1997, with Bob Rock producing once again, Re-Load's initial creative birth came during Load writing and recording sessions. Do not, however, begin to be fooled. Re-Load is neither a re-peat, a re-hash, nor a re-claiming of 'old' material.

"I was very adamant that we would have two records which would balance out with each other, not an A record and a B record," says Lars Ulrich. "They would be two records you would be able to put up against each other as strong, equal records from one songwriting and recording session. We wrote 27 songs, 1 to 27, and we recorded 27 songs, 1 to 27."

When Metallica entered The Plant in May of 1995, the idea was to record all 27 songs they had written and release them as a double album. Over the course of the next six months, Load was developed as a double album project. The decision to split the Load recordings into equal-strength siblings was made in January 1996. The deadline clock was ticking, burnout was a fear, Lollapalooza had been offered, and Metallica weren't pompous or farty enough to make a double studio album just yet. Besides, the seeds of a creative acceleration had already been sown, so why rush anything?

Let Metallica explain the story behind Re-Load. . . .

James: I remember walking into the studio, hearing Kirk playing rhythm guitar during the Load sessions and thinking, "Hmmm, things are gonna change and why fight this? How about if I jump on and use my energy in a more positive way and really make this whole thing work." At the end of the day it's a lot less stress, and you get more creative things.

Kirk: Two years down the line you're a better, more comfortable musician. Now we have the perspective to say which certain things worked and didn't work.

Jason: We were all familiar with these songs; they came to our hands more easily and the creative flow overall was the best I can remember. We all had our own rooms set up; James had his guitar equipment and cabs set up in three different

rooms just to get the metal sound, the sound of Metallica. My room had the bass real loud with a sub-woofer system that I could put my feet up, which allowed me to feel the notes as I play them, just like I do live.

Kirk: That's the way we've always done it, and that's the way we'll probably always do it. We could get together in a room and play live, but being the perfectionists we are, there's no way we could be satisfied (like that). We're our own worst critics. What would probably do for 99 percent of the world will not do for us.

Bob Rock (Producer): Lyrically *Re-Load's* the strongest yet, and I'm sure everyone will argue with me but James just gets better and better. The big difference between Metallica and the bands they initially came from, the one thing that makes them even more special, is the lyrical content.

James: I just hate the fact that those guys say at the end of the day, "It all comes down to the lyrics, the melody, what you're gonna do." It's like, F**k, I hate that. We're a f***ing band. You could have some awesome lyrics and put them on some shit song. This is a band effort.

Kirk: I heard this one song, and I thought, "Oh yeah, it sounds kinda happy" from an instrumental point of view. Then I read James' lyrics and Jesus Christ, it turned the whole song around. I've been talking to him about how great I think the lyrics are, how much it's helped me to get a better grasp on the moods and emotions behind the songs.

James: They're a lot darker—if we can get darker, that is—a lot sadder in many ways. It's not just about me, it's seeing a little more of what's going around us [in the world].

Jason: Basically it's all going to come out, it's gonna be stronger than ever, it's gonna sound good, and all the creative shit we threw on will find it's way through somehow.

Lars: As long as there is a musical vision and result in this band that works, everything else is irrelevant. What people think of the way we look, what people think of the way we dress, what people think of what we say, what people think of album covers, what people think of pictures, what people think of any of the above becomes completely irrelevant.

For 17 years, Metallica have done what they wanted to do. The release of Re-Load *continues that tradition. As James says, "We play music, and you either like that music or you don't. And we do." It's the only thing, at this stage, that you really need to know about Metallica.*

–Steffan Chirazi

FUEL

**Words and Music by James Hetfield,
Lars Ulrich and Kirk Hammett**

So gim-me fuel, gim-me fire, gim-me that which I de-sire.

Ooh,   yeah.

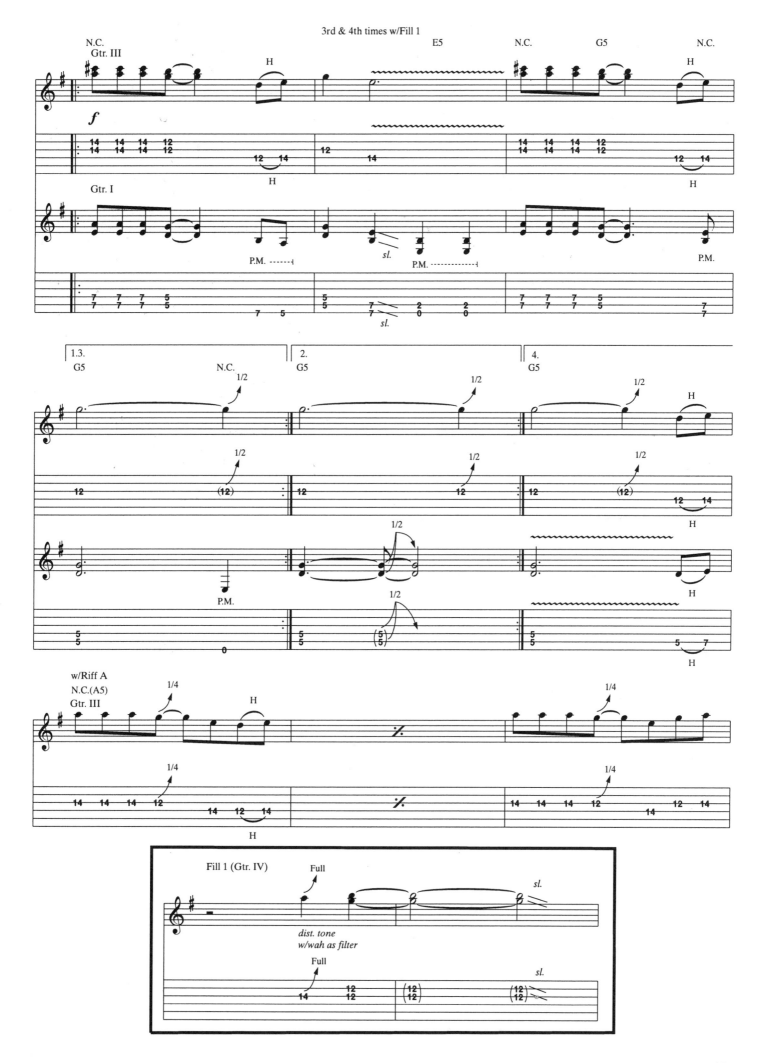

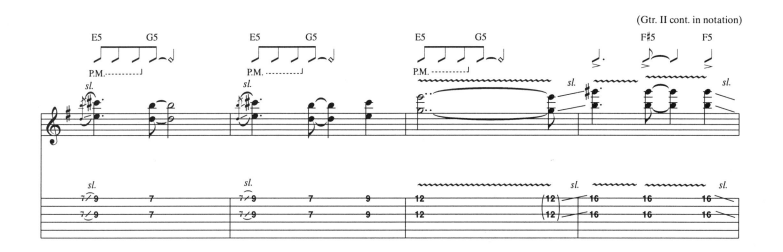

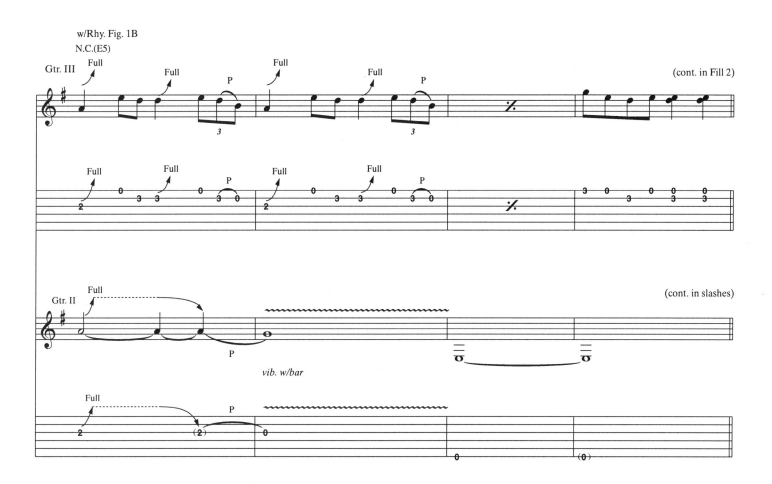

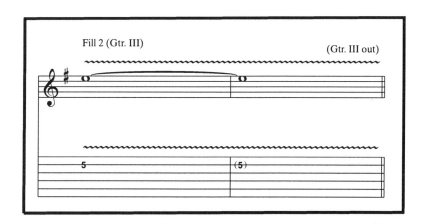

Additional Lyrics

3. Turn on beyond the bone.
   Swallow future, spit out home,
   Burn your face upon the chrome.
   Yeah, oh yeah.

4. Take the corner, join the crash.
   Headlights. (Head on.) Headlines.
   Another junkie lives too fast,
   Yeah, lives way too fast, fast, fast, woh. *(To Chorus)*

THE MEMORY REMAINS

Words and Music by
James Hetfield and Lars Ulrich

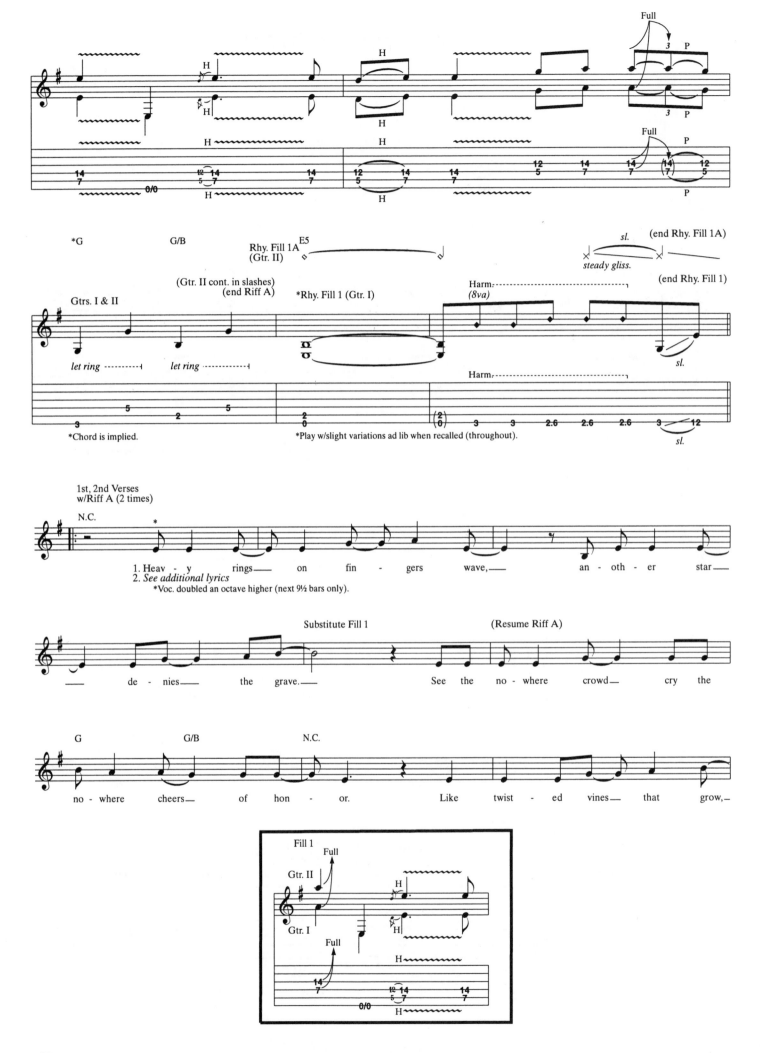

For - tune, fame,— mir - ror vain,—

gone in - sane,— but the mem - o - ry— re - mains.—

*E played by bass only.

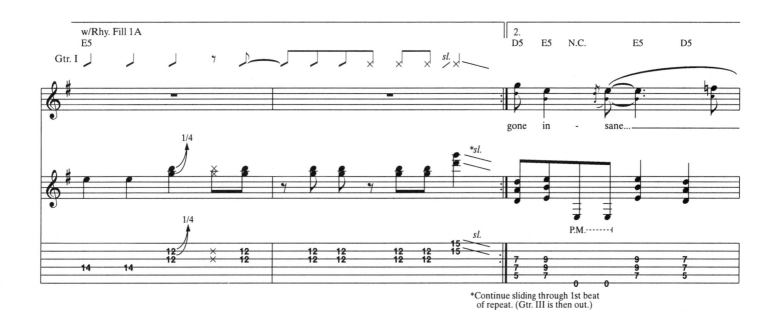

*Continue sliding through 1st beat of repeat. (Gtr. III is then out.)

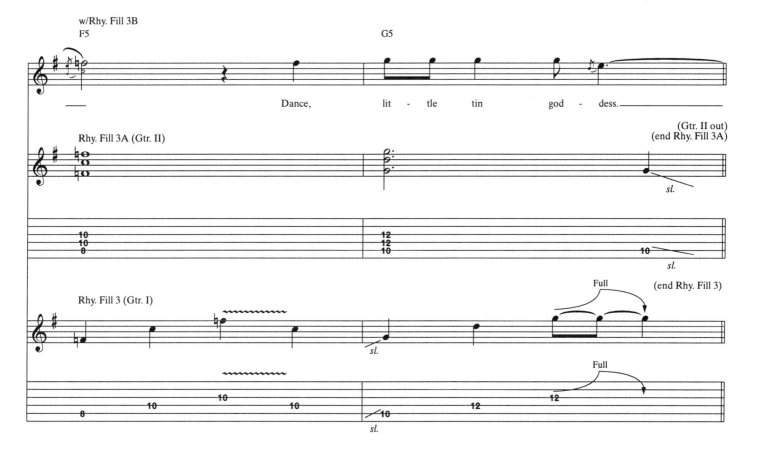

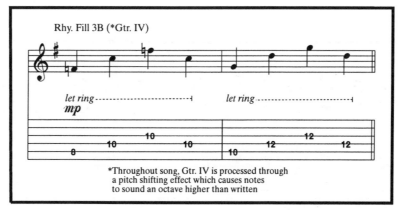

*Throughout song, Gtr. IV is processed through a pitch shifting effect which causes notes to sound an octave higher than written

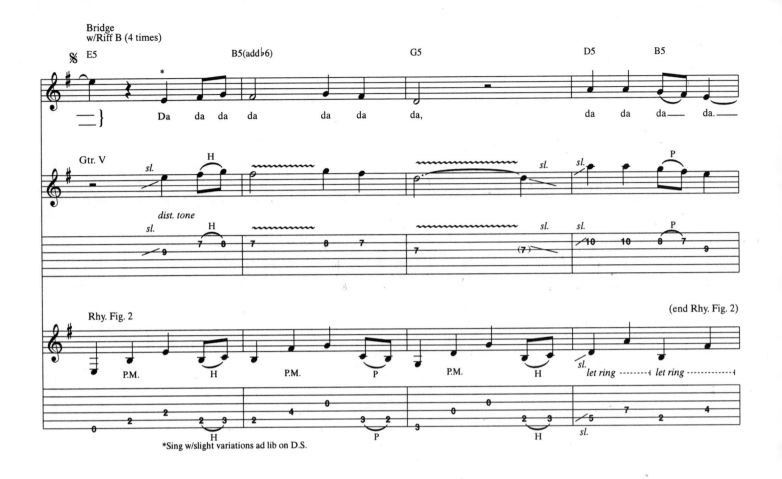

*Sing w/slight variations ad lib on D.S.

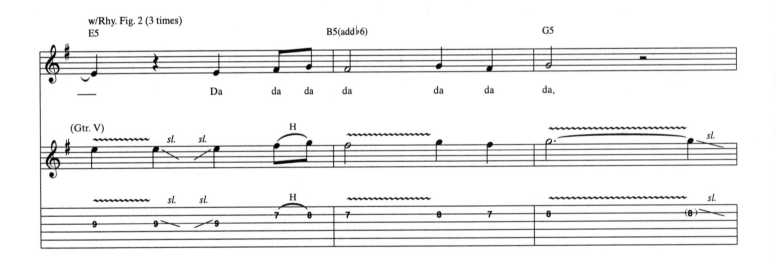

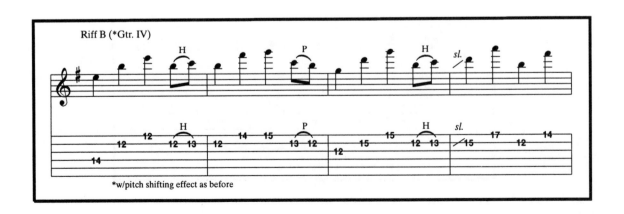

*w/pitch shifting effect as before

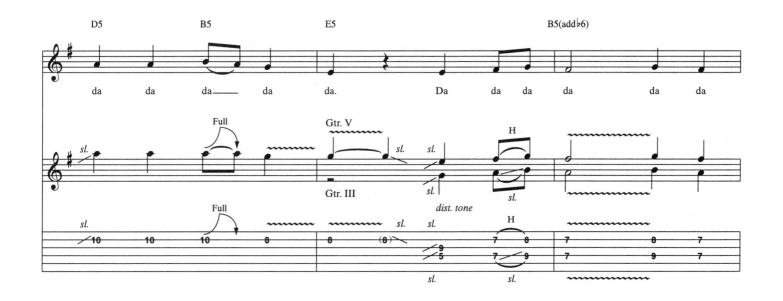

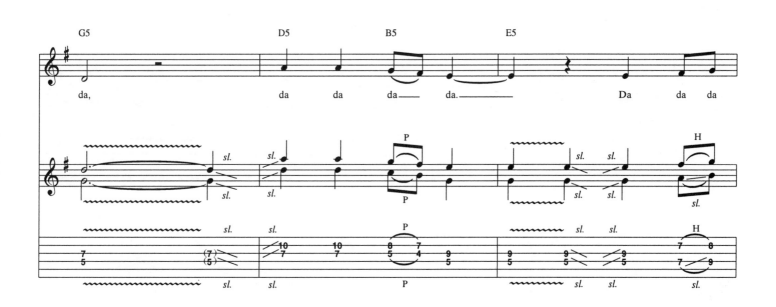

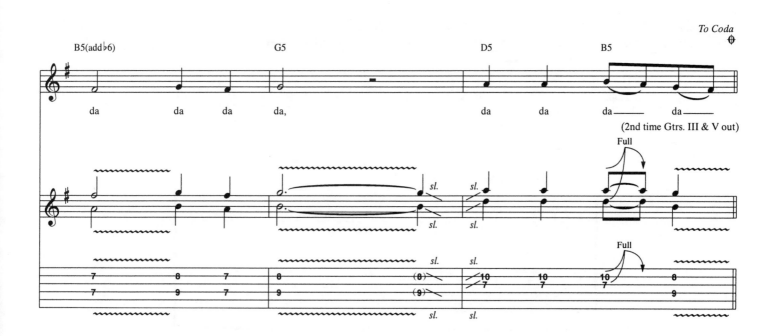

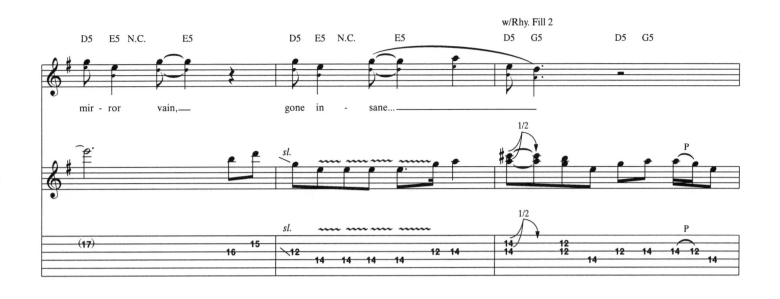

mir - ror vain,— gone in - sane..._____

For - tune, fame,— mir - ror vain,— gone in - sane,— but the

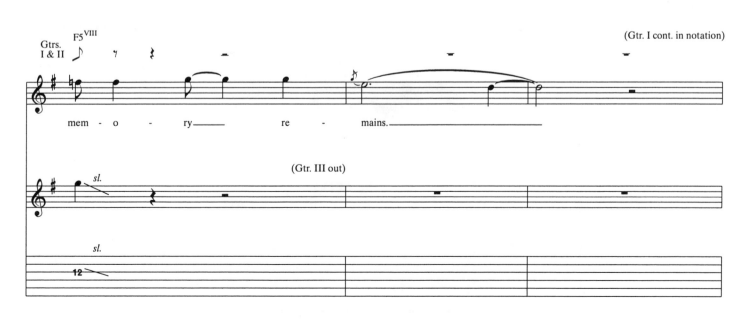

mem - o - ry_____ re - mains._____

Guitar solo
w/Riff A (1st 3 bars only)

N.C.

w/Fill 4

D5　　E5

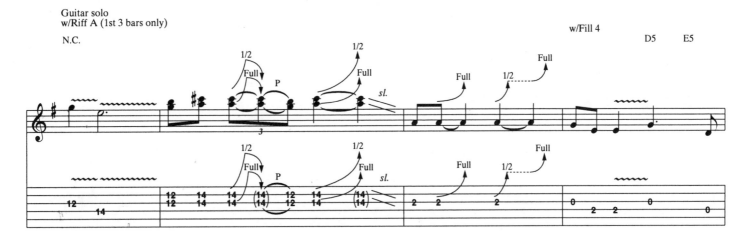

w/Riff A (1st 3 bars only)

N.C.

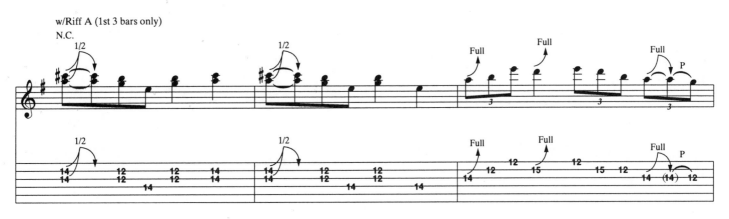

w/Rhy. Fills 3, 3A & 3B

D.S. al Coda

F5

G5

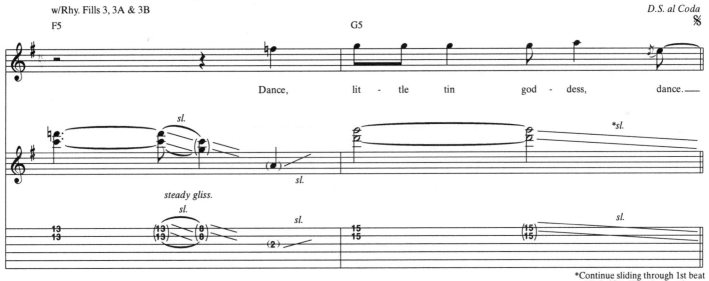

Dance,　lit - tle　tin　god - dess,　dance. ——

*Continue sliding through 1st beat
of D.S. (Gtr. III is then out.)

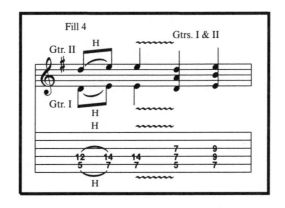

Fill 4

Gtrs. I & II

Gtr. II

Gtr. I

*Gtr. IV gradually fades out, substituting Fill 5 for 4th bar of Riff B,
2nd and 4th times only. Gtr. IV continues playing in 4/4 regardless of vocal
singing in 2/4 for one bar.

Additional Lyrics

2. Heavy rings hold cigarettes
Up to lips that time forgets
While the Hollywood sun sets
Behind your back.
And can't the band play on?
Just listen, they play my song.
Ash to ash, dust to dust,
Fade to black. *(To Chorus)*

DEVIL'S DANCE

Words and Music by
James Hetfield and Lars Ulrich

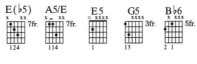

Tune down one whole step:

⑥=D ③=F
⑤=G ②=A
④=C ①=D

Moderately slow Rock ♩ = 96

(Bass & drums)

N.C.(E5)

Intro · Gtr. I · *dist. tone w/delay* · ƒ · P.M. · 1/2

Rhy. Fig. 1 (Gtr. I) · P.M. · (cont. in slashes) Gtr. II · 1/4 · H · P.M. · *dist. tone* · 1/4

(end Rhy. Fig. 1) · w/Rhy. Fig. 1 (3½ times) · Full · 1/4 · H · sl.

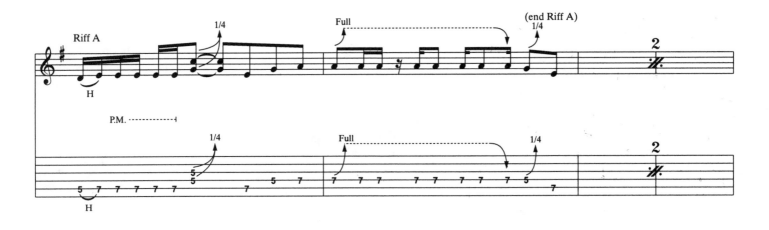

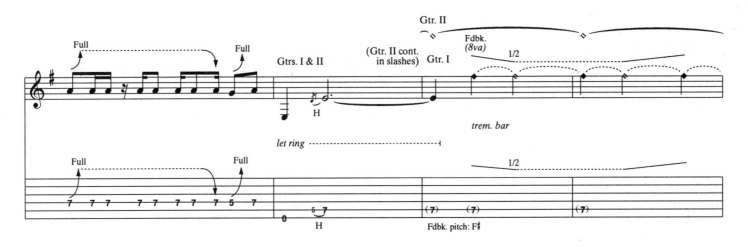

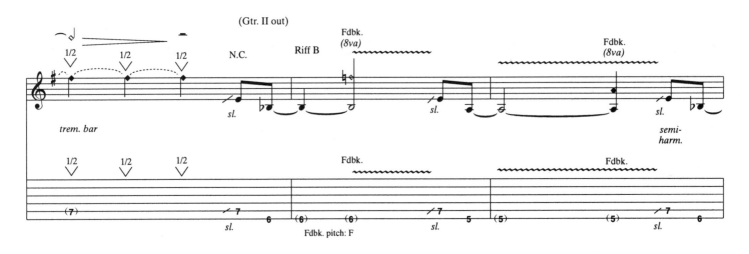

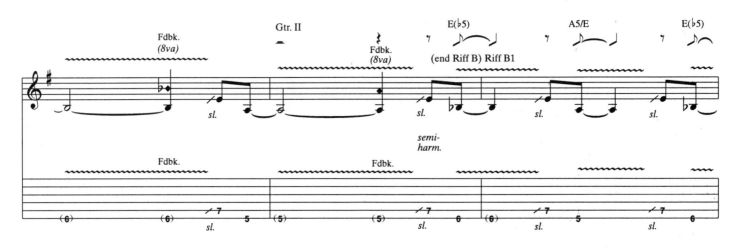

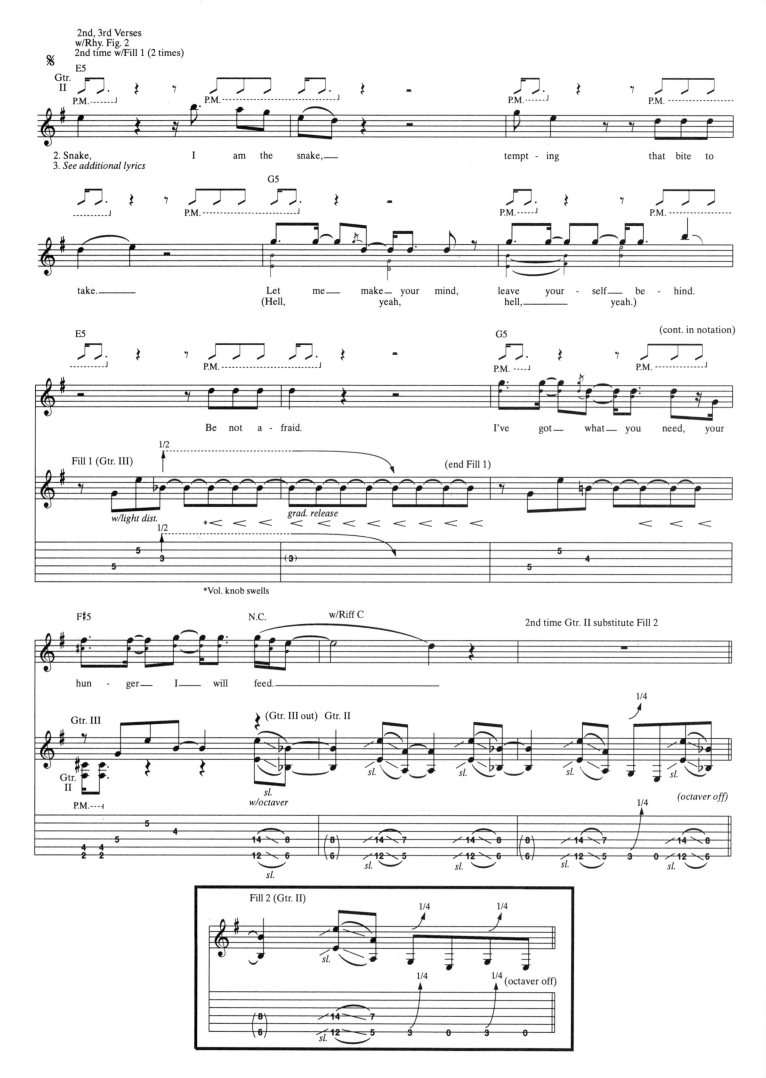

2nd, 3rd Verses
w/Rhy. Fig. 2
2nd time w/Fill 1 (2 times)

2. Snake, I am the snake, tempt-ing that bite to
3. *See additional lyrics*

take. Let me make your mind, leave your-self be-hind.
(Hell, yeah, hell, yeah.)

Be not a-fraid. I've got what you need, your

Fill 1 (Gtr. III)   (end Fill 1)

w/light dist.   grad. release

*Vol. knob swells

hun - ger I will feed.

Gtr. III   (Gtr. III out) Gtr. II   2nd time Gtr. II substitute Fill 2

Gtr.
II

sl.
w/octaver   sl.   sl.   sl.   sl.

(octaver off)

Fill 2 (Gtr. II)

sl.   (octaver off)

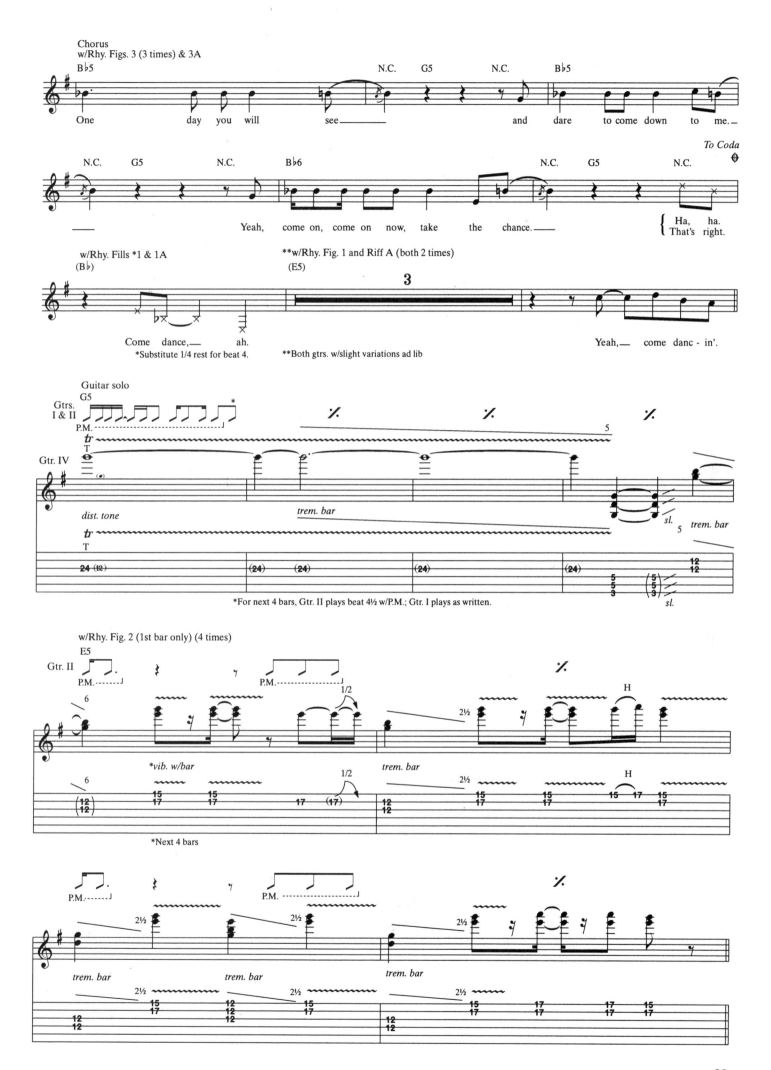

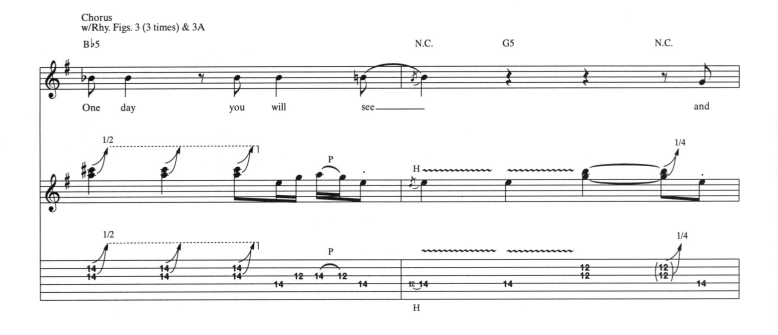

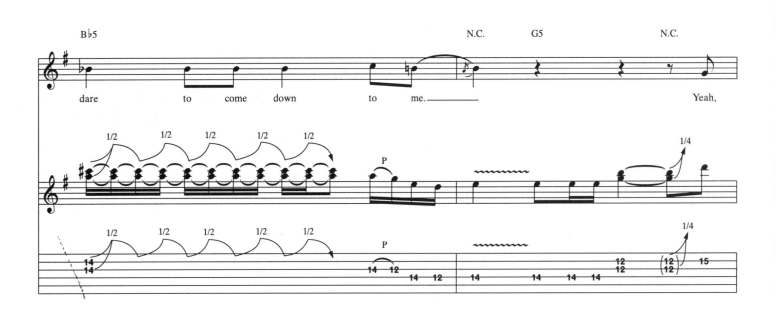

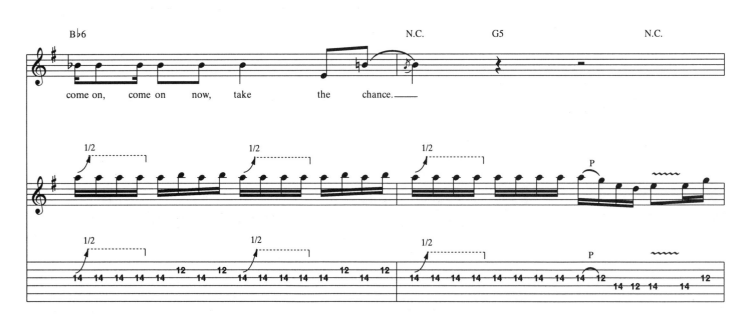

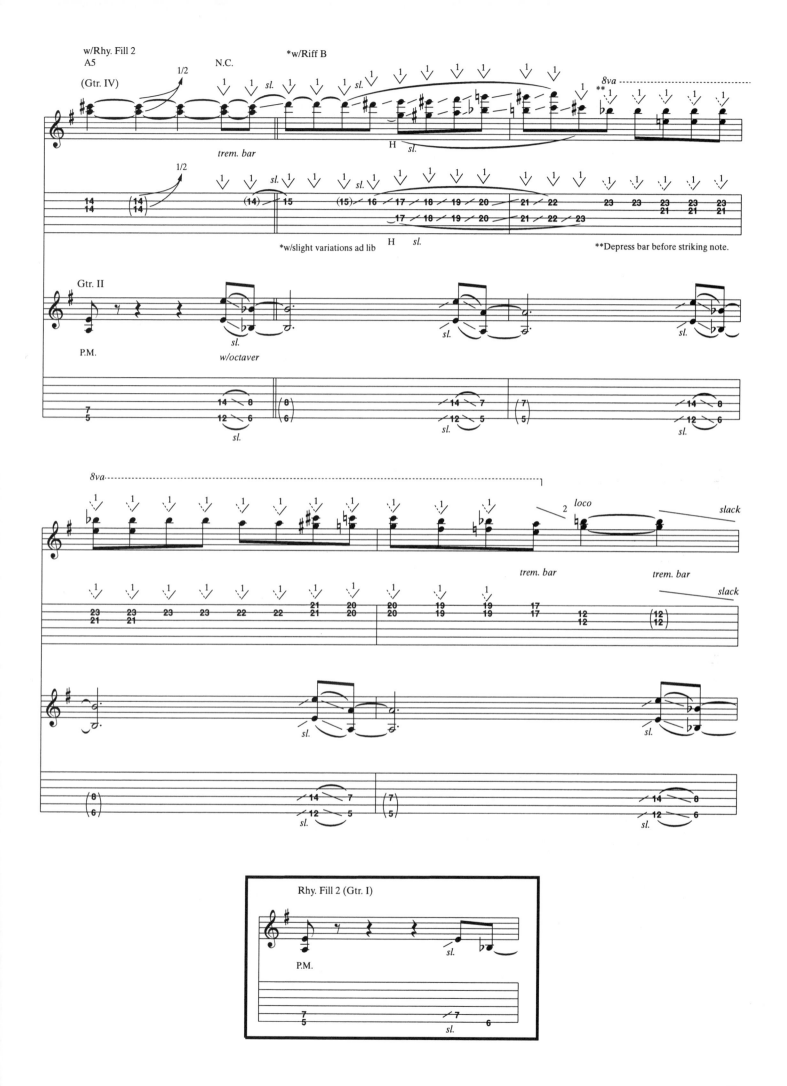

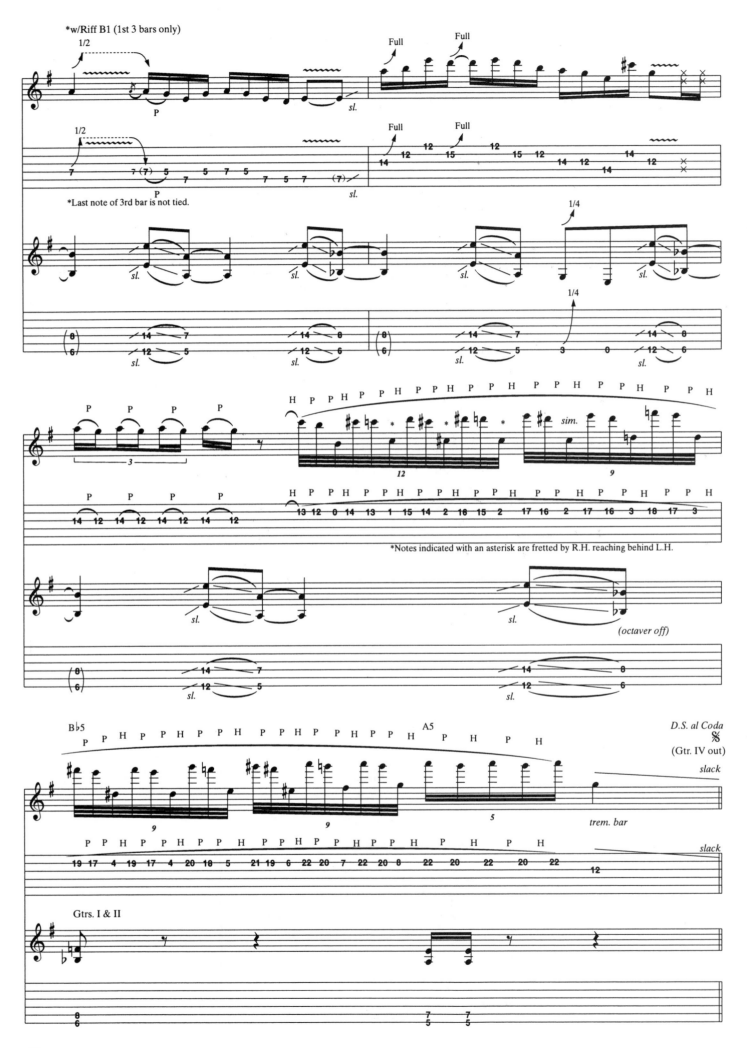

42

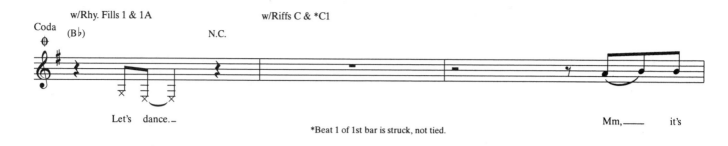

*Beat 1 of 1st bar is struck, not tied.

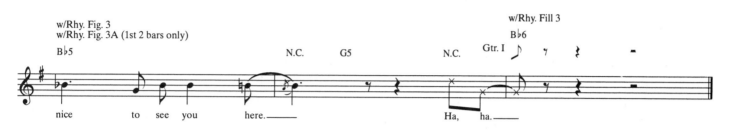

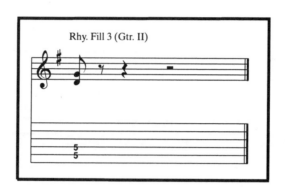

Rhy. Fill 3 (Gtr. II)

Additional Lyrics

3. Yeah, I feel you too,
   Feel those things you do.
   In your eyes I see a fire that burns
   To free the you that's wanting through.
   Deep inside you know
   The seeds I plant will grow. *(To Chorus)*

THE UNFORGIVEN II

Words and Music by James Hetfield,
Lars Ulrich and Kirk Hammett

46

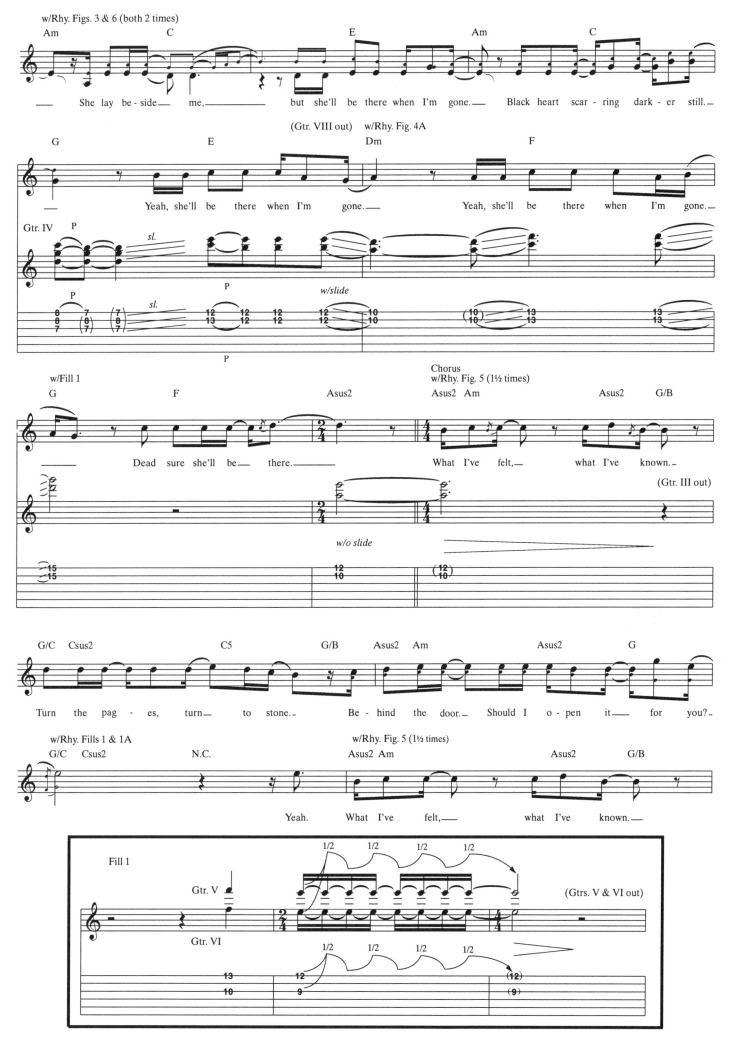

49

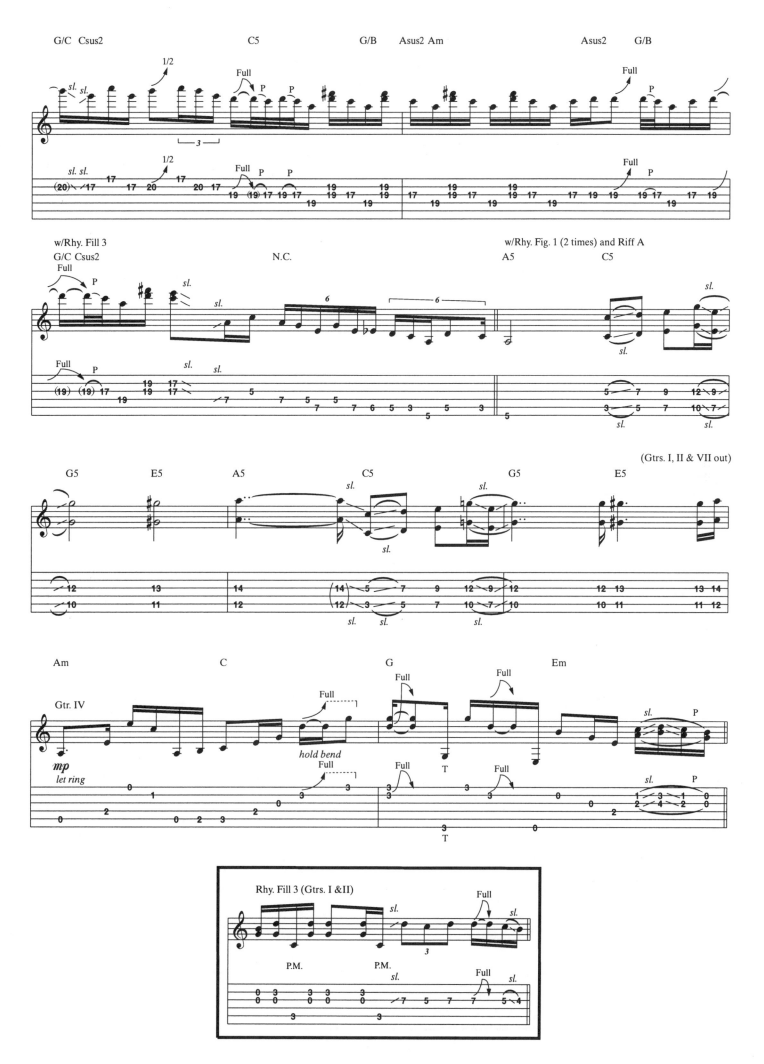

Better Than You

Words and Music by
James Hetfield and Lars Ulrich

*Notes to right of slashes played by bass only.

**Words and Music by James Hetfield,
Lars Ulrich and Kirk Hammett**

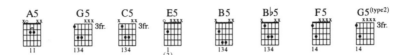

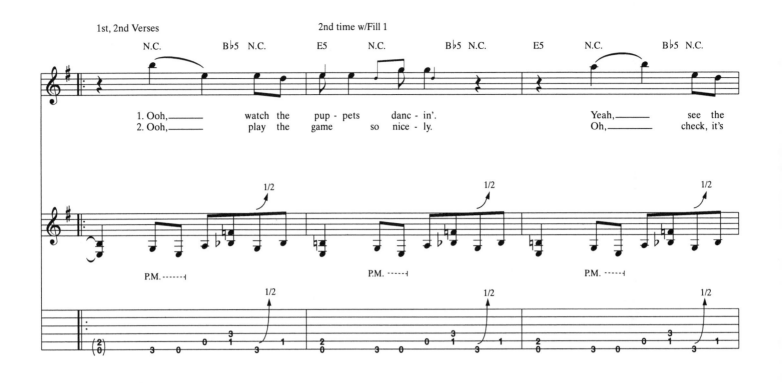

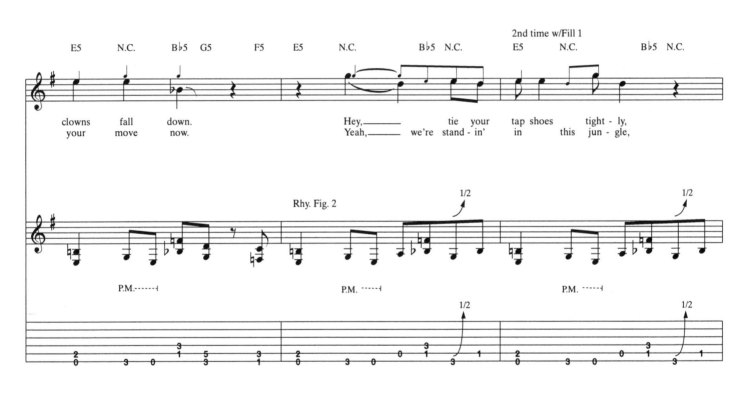

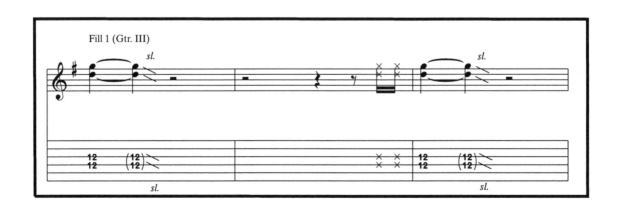

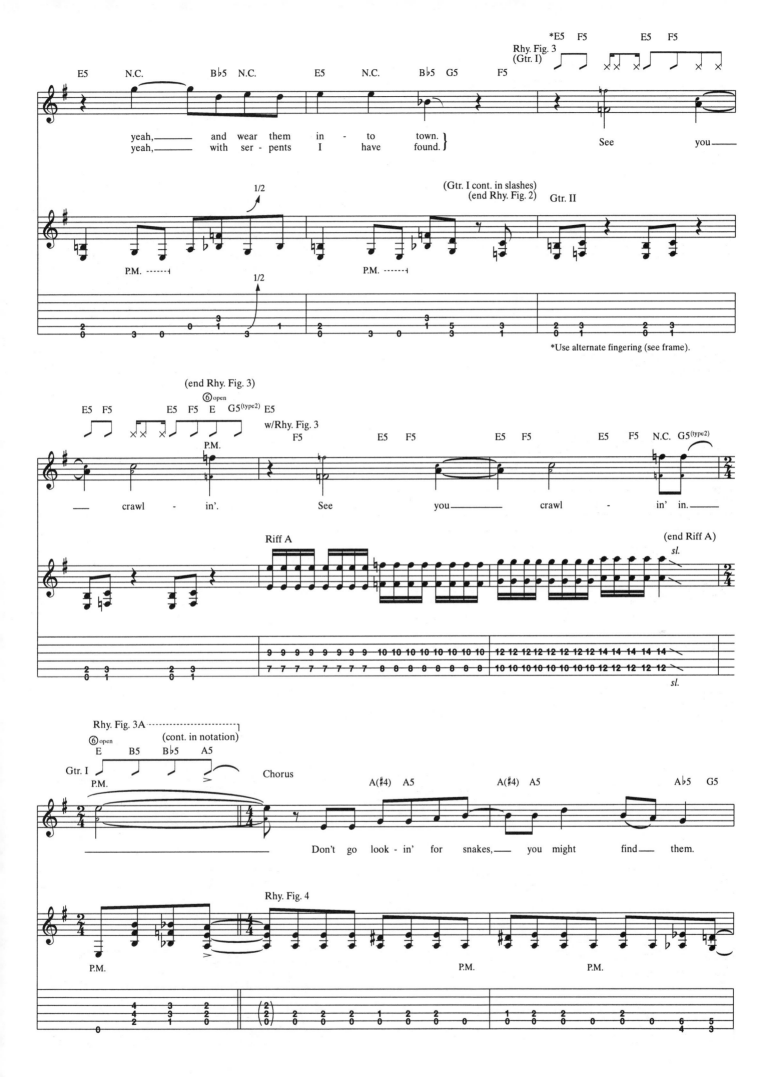

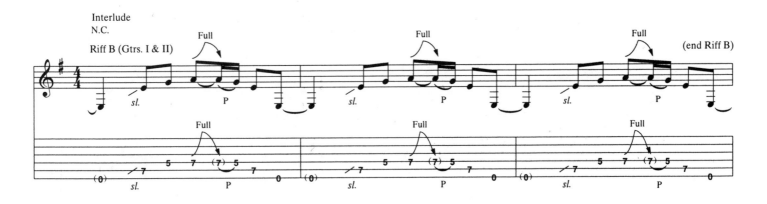

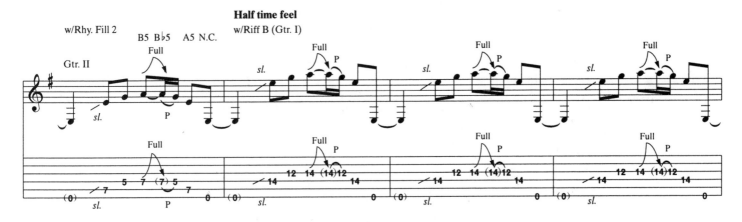

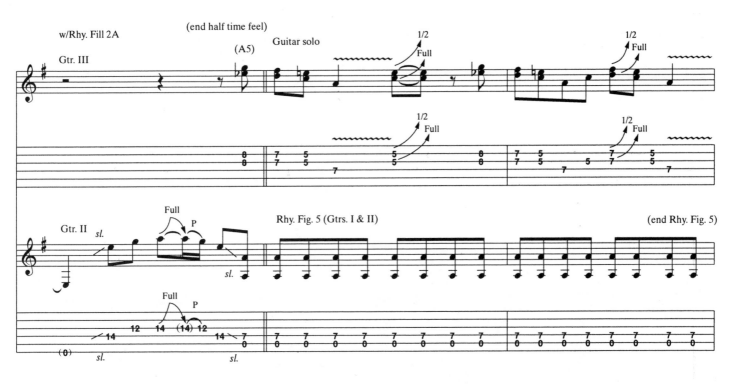

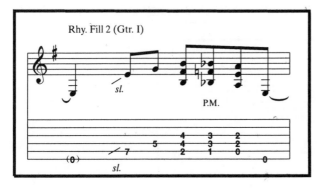

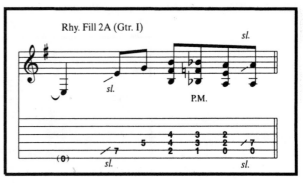

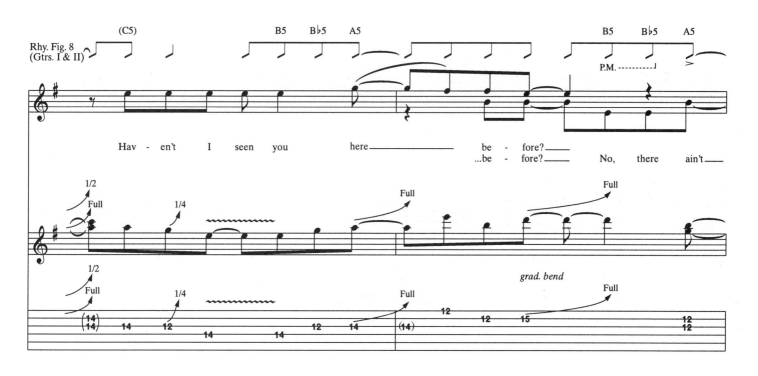

Hav - en't I seen you here _____ be - fore? _____
...be - fore? _____ No, there ain't _____

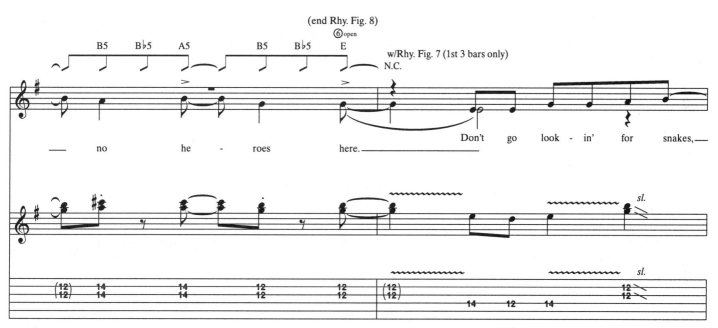

— no he - roes here. _____
Don't go look - in' for snakes, _____

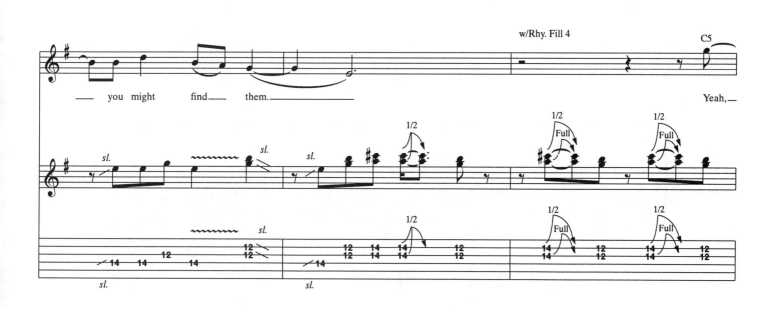

— you might find _____ them. _____
Yeah, _____

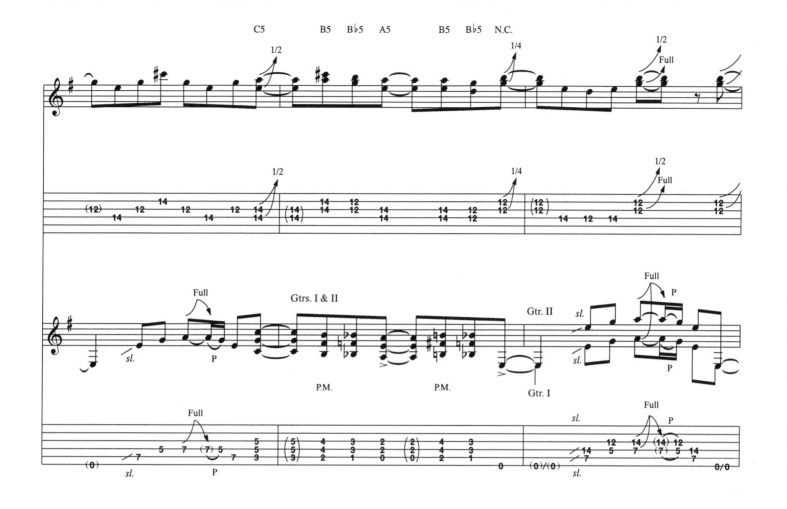

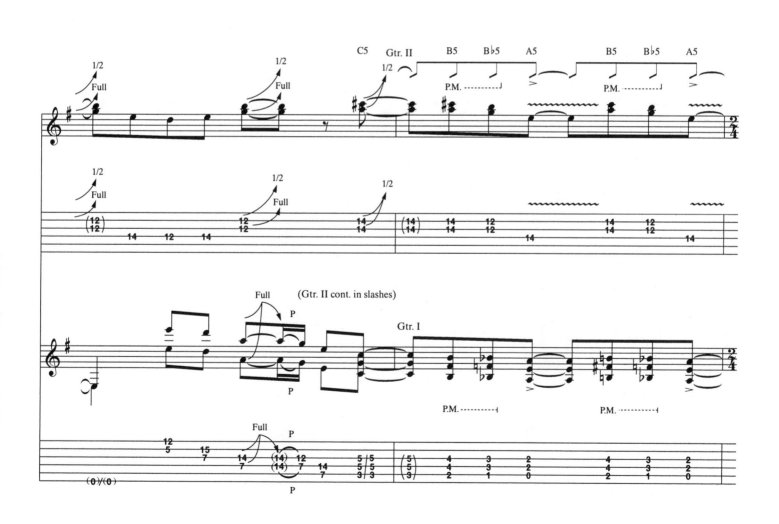

CARPE DIEM BABY

Words and Music by James Hetfield,
Lars Ulrich and Kirk Hammett

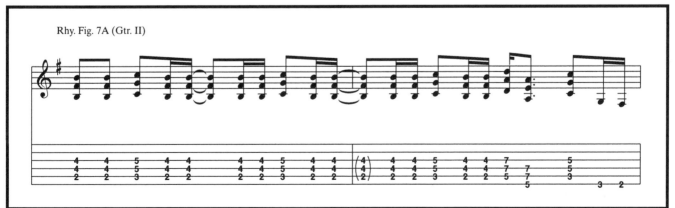

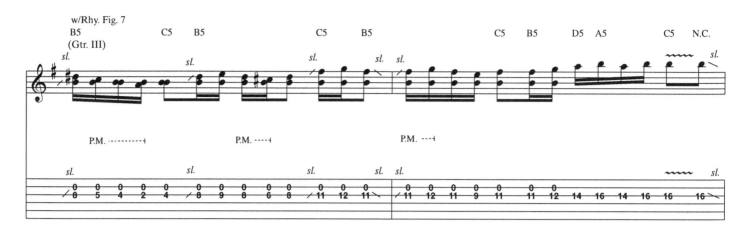

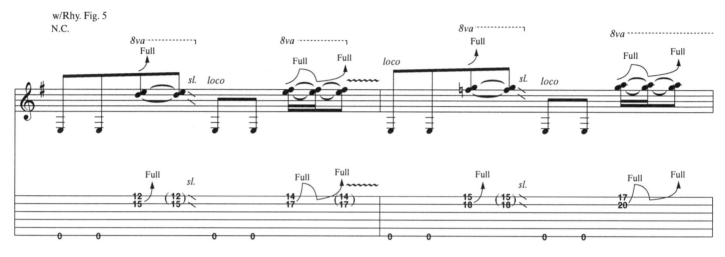

Dsus2   E5 F5   C5   D5 E5   D5 E5 F5 E5 N.C.   Dsus2   E5 F5   C5

bleed the day and break the rule.___ Hug the curve, lose the time, tear the map and shoot the sign.___

Coda   Gtr. II   A5   Cadd9

Come squeeze and suck the day.___

Gtr. I

A5   ⑥ open   E   F5

Come make me miss___ you.___ Come car - pe di - em, ba -

P.M.

Outro
w/Rhy. Fig. 4
N.C.

by.___ Come car - pe di - em, ba -   by.

Gtr. III

88

Additional Lyrics

2. Draw lead, piss wine,
   Sink teeth, all mine.
   Stoke fire, break neck,
   Suffer through this, cheat on death.
   Hug the curve, lose the time,
   Tear the map and shoot the sign. *(To Pre-chorus)*

BAD SEED

Words and Music by James Hetfield,
Lars Ulrich and Kirk Hammett

91

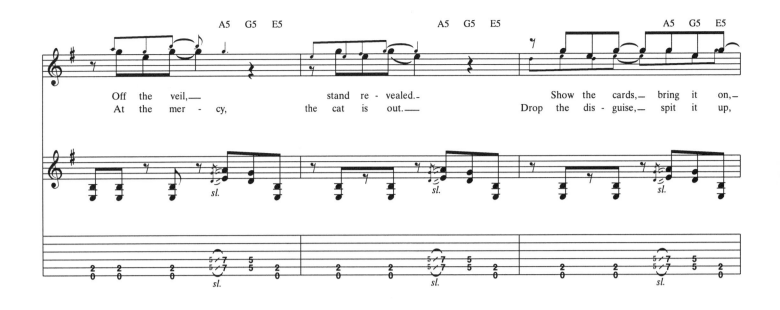

Off the veil,— stand re - vealed.— Show the cards,— bring it on,—
At the mer - cy, the cat is out.— Drop the dis - guise,— spit it up,

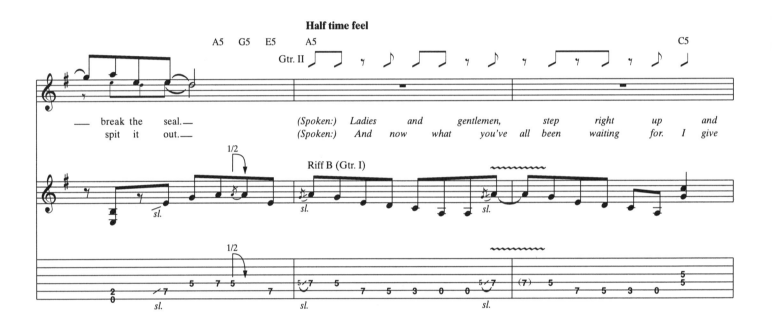

Half time feel

Gtr. II

— break the seal.—
spit it out.—

(Spoken:) Ladies and gentlemen, step right up and
(Spoken:) And now what you've all been waiting for. I give

Riff B (Gtr. I)

(cont. in notation)

see the man who told the truth.
you he who suffers the truth.

(end Riff B)

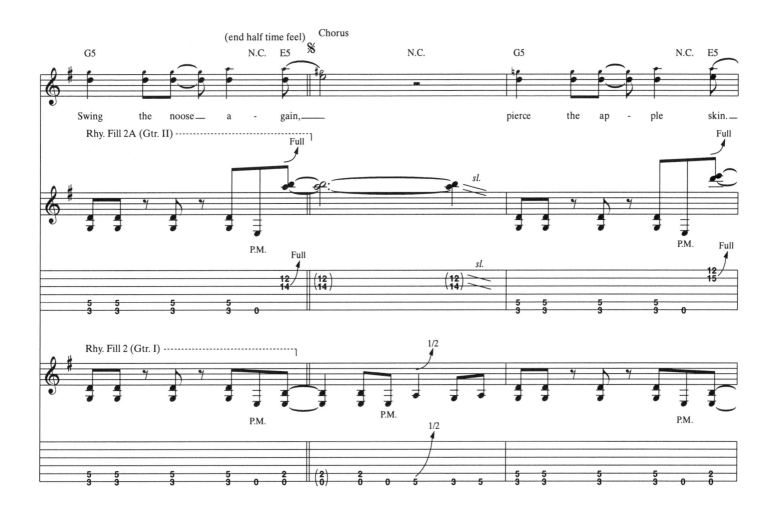

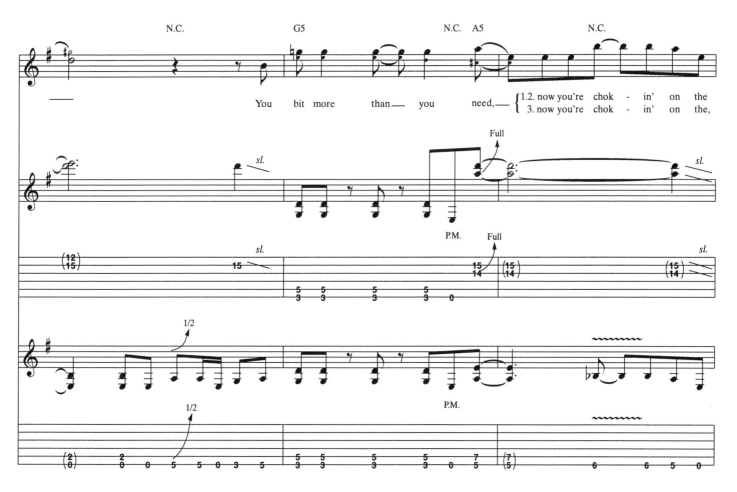

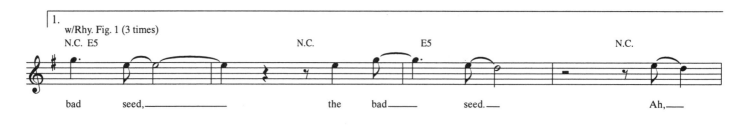

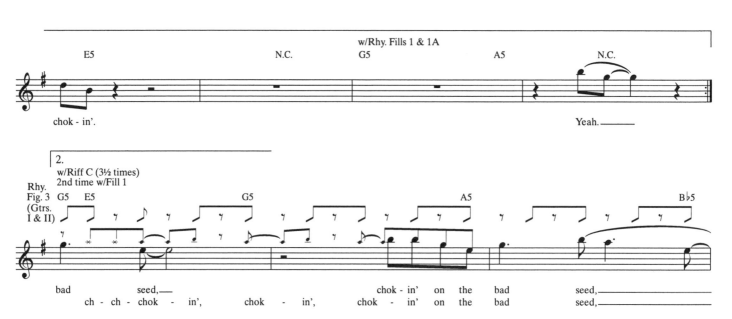

bad seed,_____ the bad_____ seed._____ Ah,_____

chok - in'. Yeah._____

bad seed,_____ chok - in' on the bad seed,_____
ch - ch - chok - in', chok - in', chok - in' on the bad seed,_____

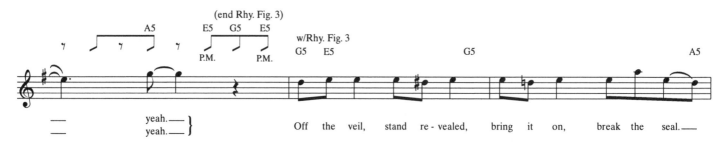

_____ yeah._____
_____ yeah._____ }

Off the veil, stand re - vealed, bring it on, break the seal._____

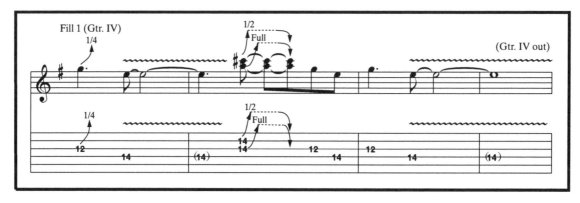

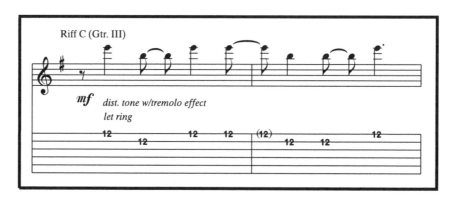

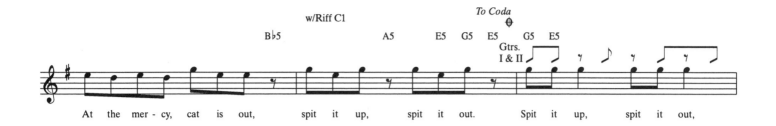

At the mer - cy, cat is out, spit it up, spit it out. Spit it up, spit it out,

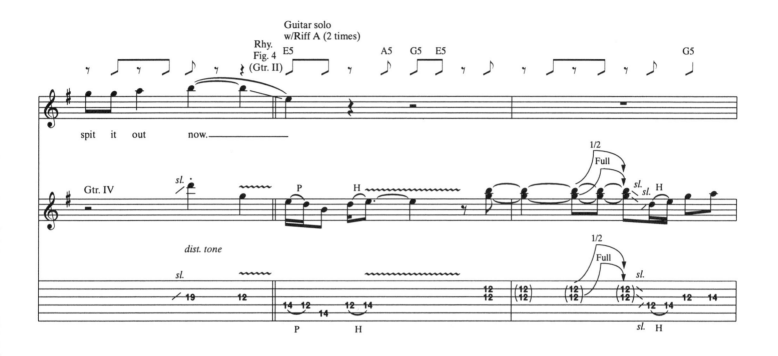

spit it out now.

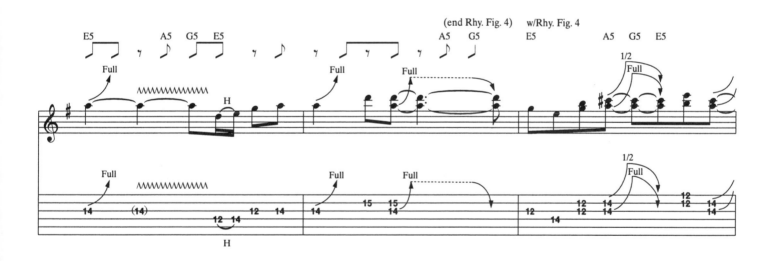

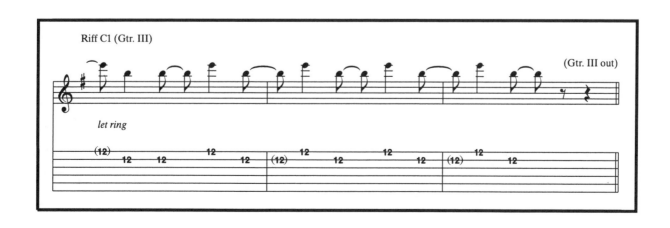

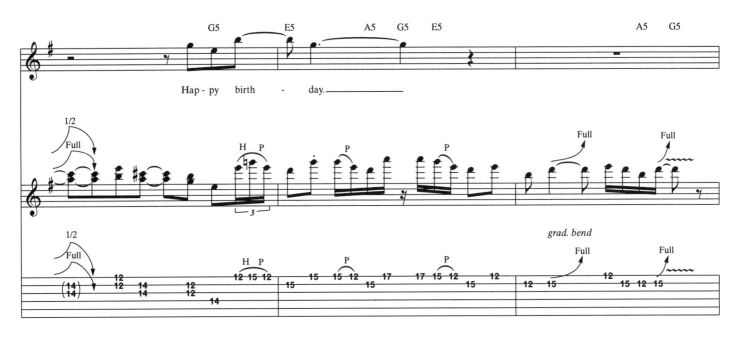

Hap - py birth - day. _____

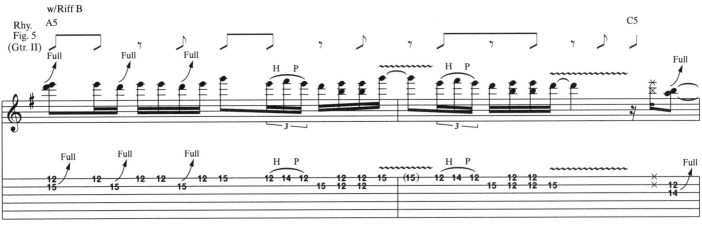

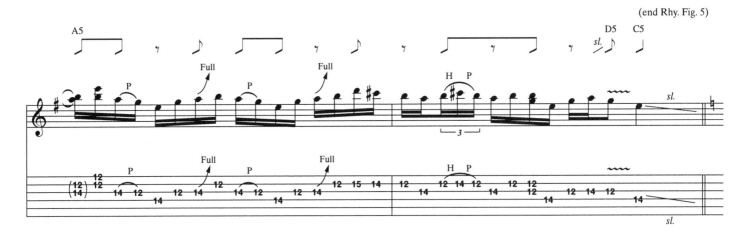

(end Rhy. Fig. 5)

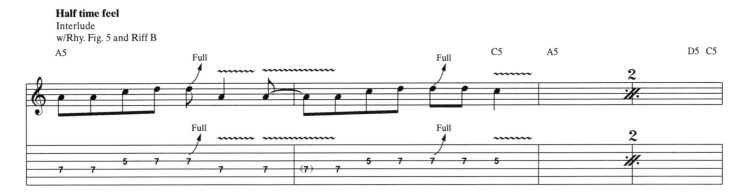

Half time feel
Interlude
w/Rhy. Fig. 5 and Riff B

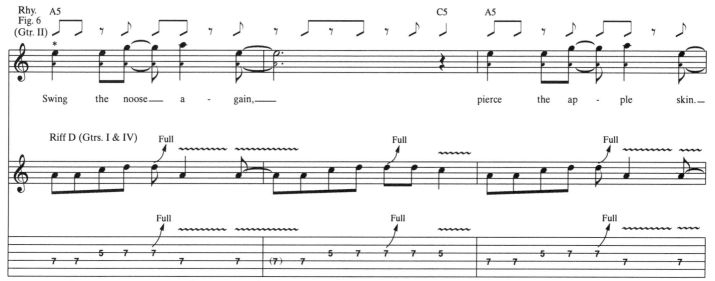

Swing the noose— a - gain,— pierce the ap - ple skin.—

*Lead voc. doubled on octave lower (next 10 bars only).

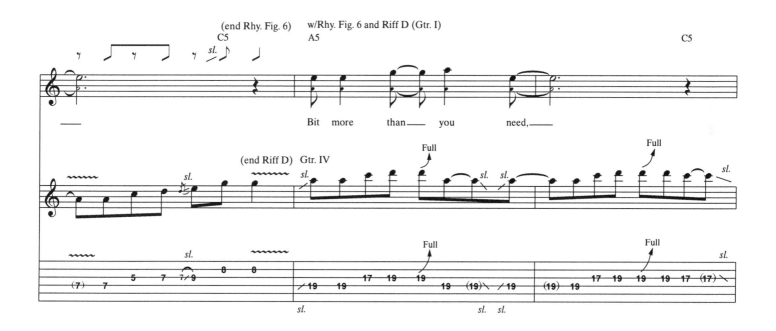

Bit more than— you need,—

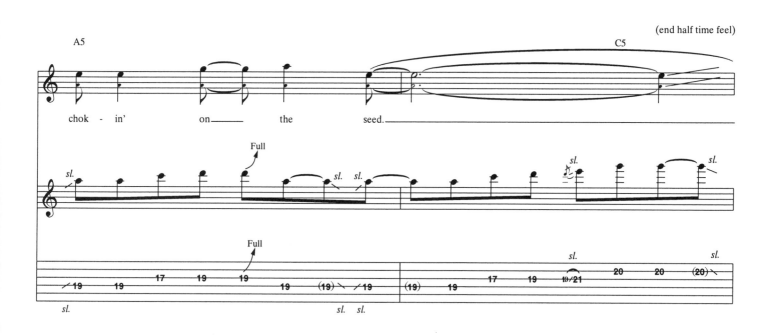

chok - in' on— the seed.—

WHERE THE WILD THINGS ARE

Words and Music by James Hetfield,
Lars Ulrich and Jason Newsted

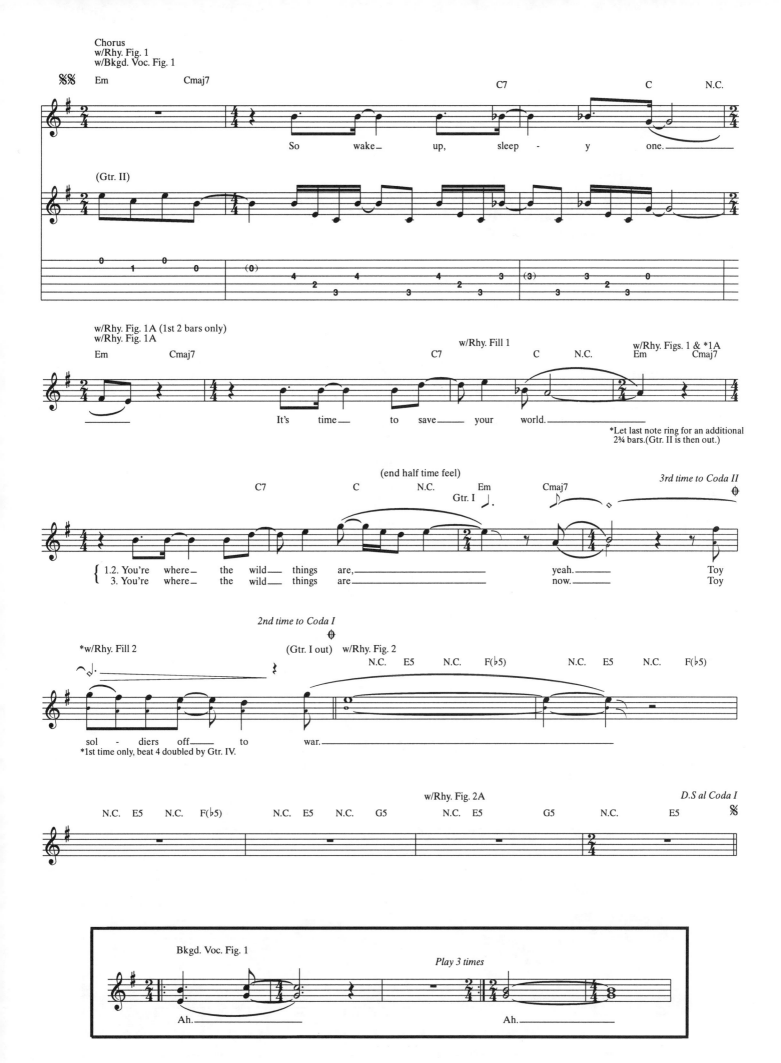

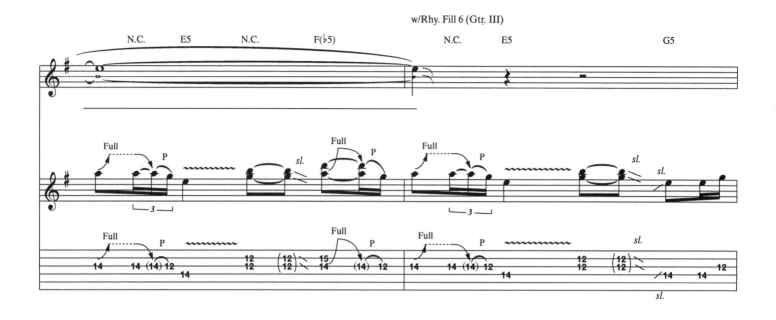

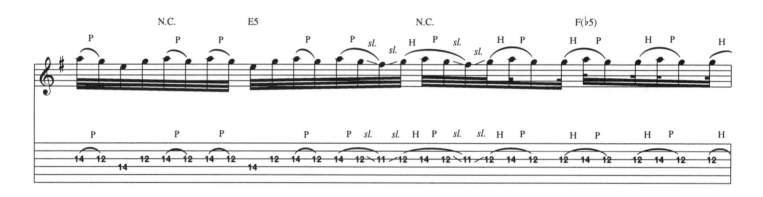

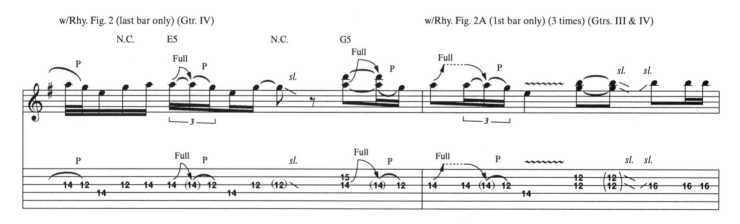

Additional Lyrics

2. Big eyes to open soon,
   Believing all under sun and moon.
   But does heaven know you're here?
   And did they give you smiles or tears?
   No, no tears. *(To Pre-chorus)*

Prince Charming

Words and Music by
James Hetfield and Lars Ulrich

110

111

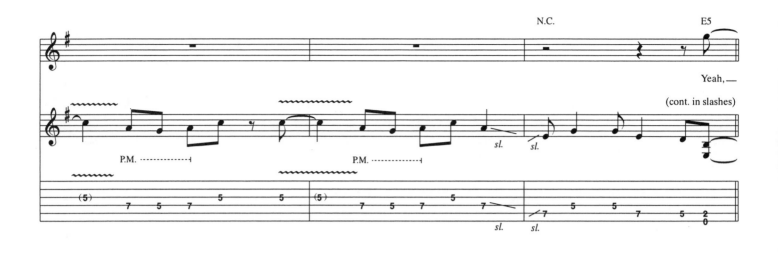

N.C.

E5

Yeah, ——

(cont. in slashes)

P.M. ─────┤

P.M. ─────┤

sl. sl.

sl. sl.

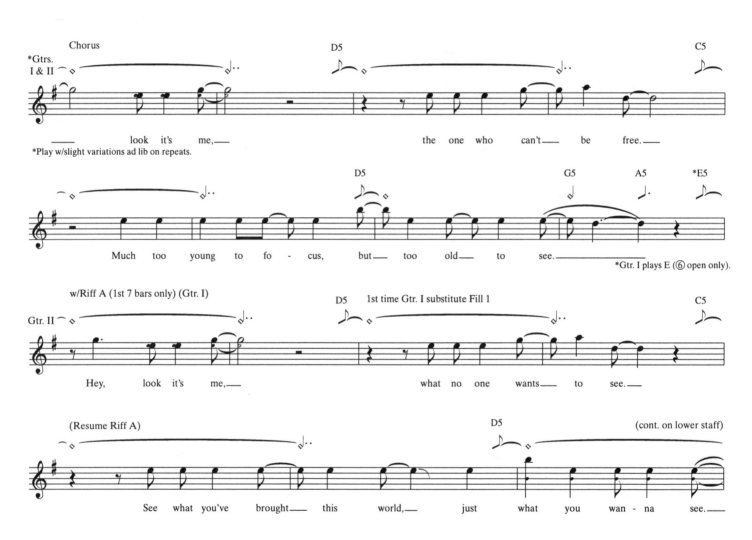

Chorus

*Gtrs.
I & II

D5

C5

—— look it's me, ——

the one who can't—— be free. ——

*Play w/slight variations ad lib on repeats.

D5

G5   A5   *E5

Much too young to fo - cus, but—— too old—— to see. ——

*Gtr. I plays E (⑥ open only).

w/Riff A (1st 7 bars only) (Gtr. I)

D5   1st time Gtr. I substitute Fill 1

C5

Gtr. II

Hey, look it's me,—— what no one wants—— to see. ——

(Resume Riff A)

D5

(cont. on lower staff)

See what you've brought—— this world,—— just what you wan - na see. ——

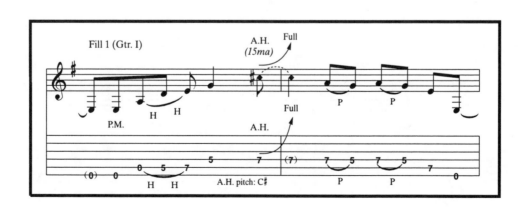

Fill 1 (Gtr. I)

A.H.
(15ma)   Full

P.M.

H   H

A.H.

Full

A.H. pitch: C#

P   P

H   H

P   P

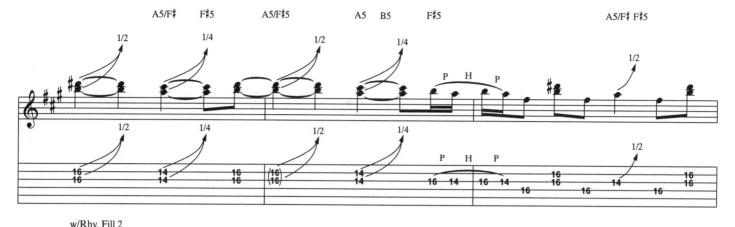

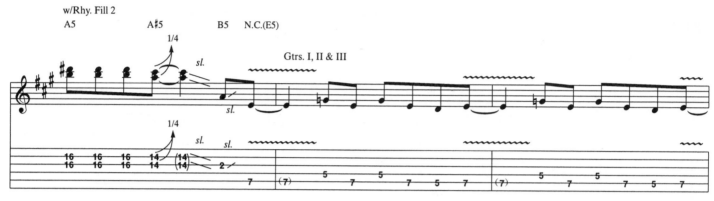

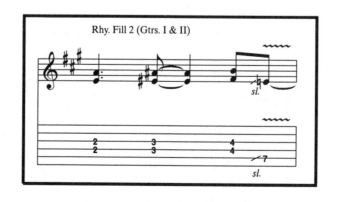

119

*Gtr. I plays E (⑥ open only).

Hey, ma! Hey, ma! Look, it's me.

Outro solo
w/Riff A (Gtr. I)

(See right

*Rock wah pedal back and forth ad lib.

Additional Lyrics

3. And he wants to be called father now.
   Me again, me.
   The marks inside your arm spell me,
   Spell only me.
   I'm the nothing face that plants the bomb
   And strolls away.
   I'm the one who doesn't look quite right
   As children play. *(To Chorus)*

4. See the black cloud overhead.
   (That's me.)
   This poison ivy chokes the tree.
   (Again it's me.)
   And I'm the filthy one on Bourbon Street
   You walk on by.
   And I'm the little boy that pushes, pushes,
   Makes them cry. *(To Chorus)*

LOW MAN'S LYRIC

Words and Music by
James Hetfield and Lars Ulrich

*Substitute cue note when
Riff A is recalled (throughout).

1st Verse
w/Rhy. Fig. 1 (2 times)
w/Riff A (4 times)

Chorus
w/Rhy. Fig. 2
2nd time w/Rhy. Fill 3

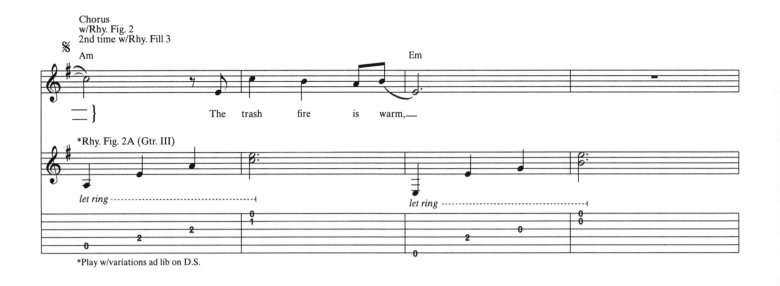

The trash fire is warm,—

*Play w/variations ad lib on D.S.

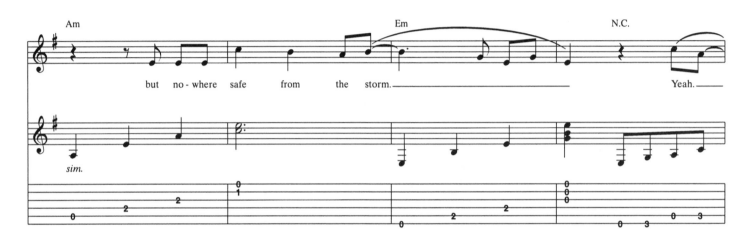

but no-where safe from the storm.————— Yeah.———

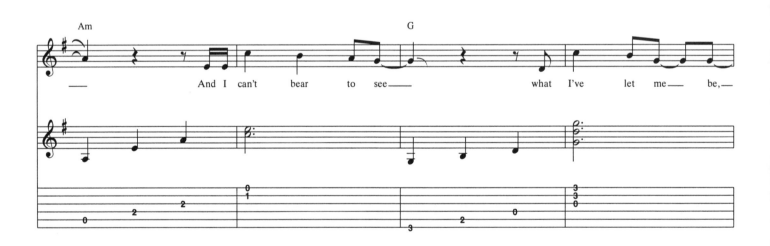

—— And I can't bear to see—— what I've let me be,—

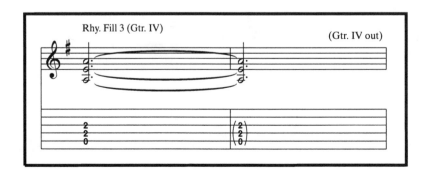

128

fess all_____ to the rain._____ But I

lie, lie straight to the mir - ror, the one I've

bro - ken to match my face.

My eyes

seek re - al - i - ty,_____ my fin - gers_____ seek my veins.

*2nd time, Gtr. I substitutes cue note (w/P.M.) and begins to fade out.

*Gtr. I tacet on repeats.
**P.M. refers to Gtr. I only.

Words and Music by
James Hetfield and Lars Ulrich

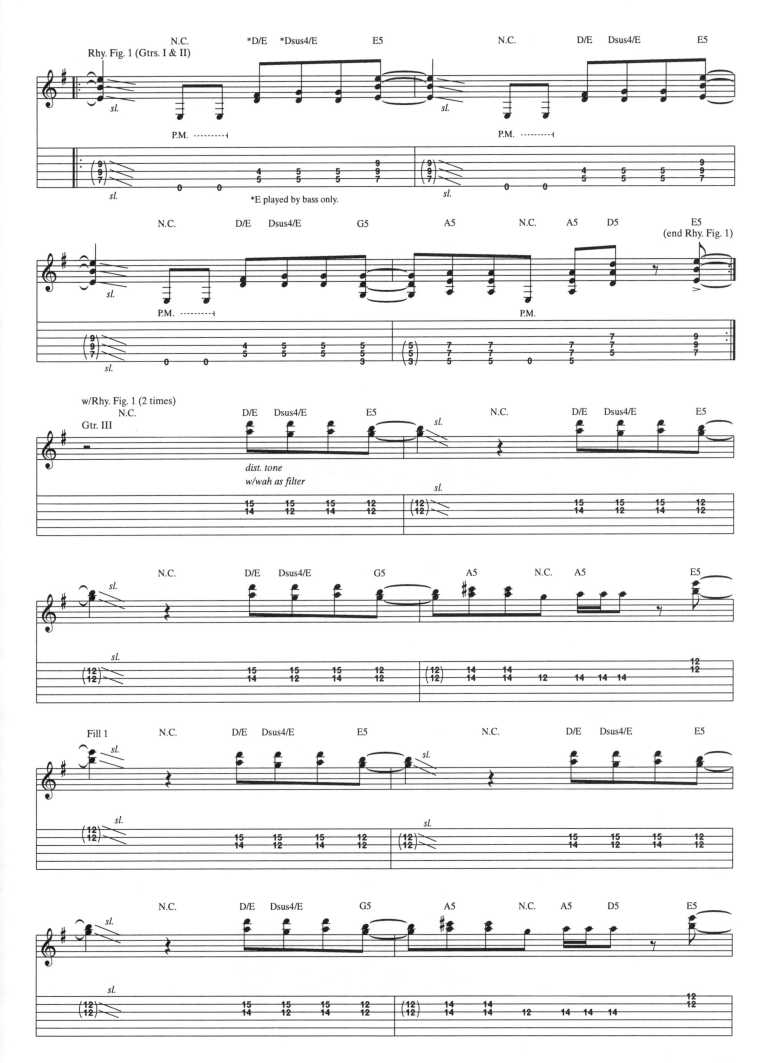

*Play w/slight variations ad lib on repeat (next 6 bars only).

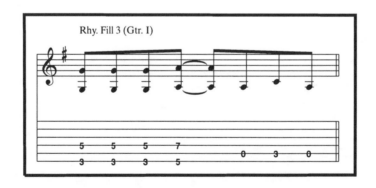

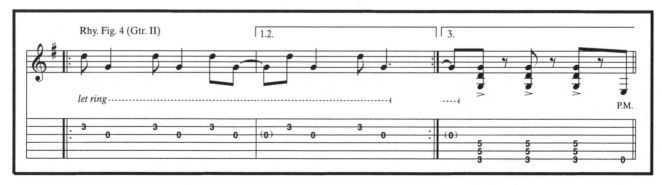

*Wah off

Half time feel

Interlude

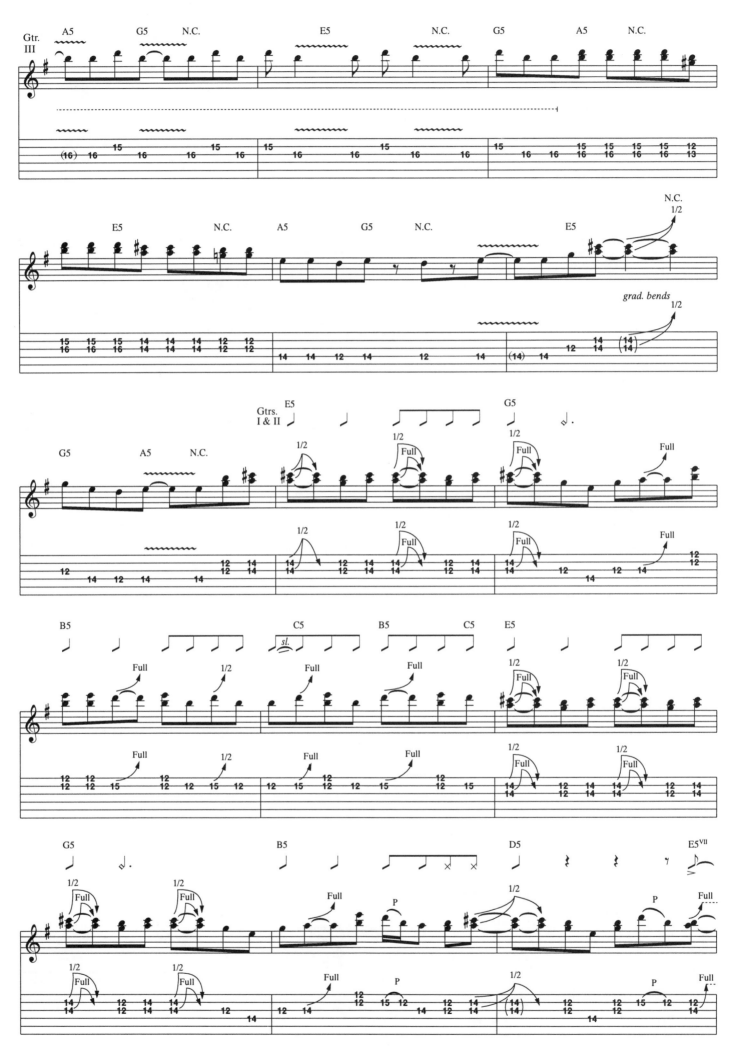

*Doubled by spoken voice (next 8 bars only).   **Bass plays E pedal till D.S.

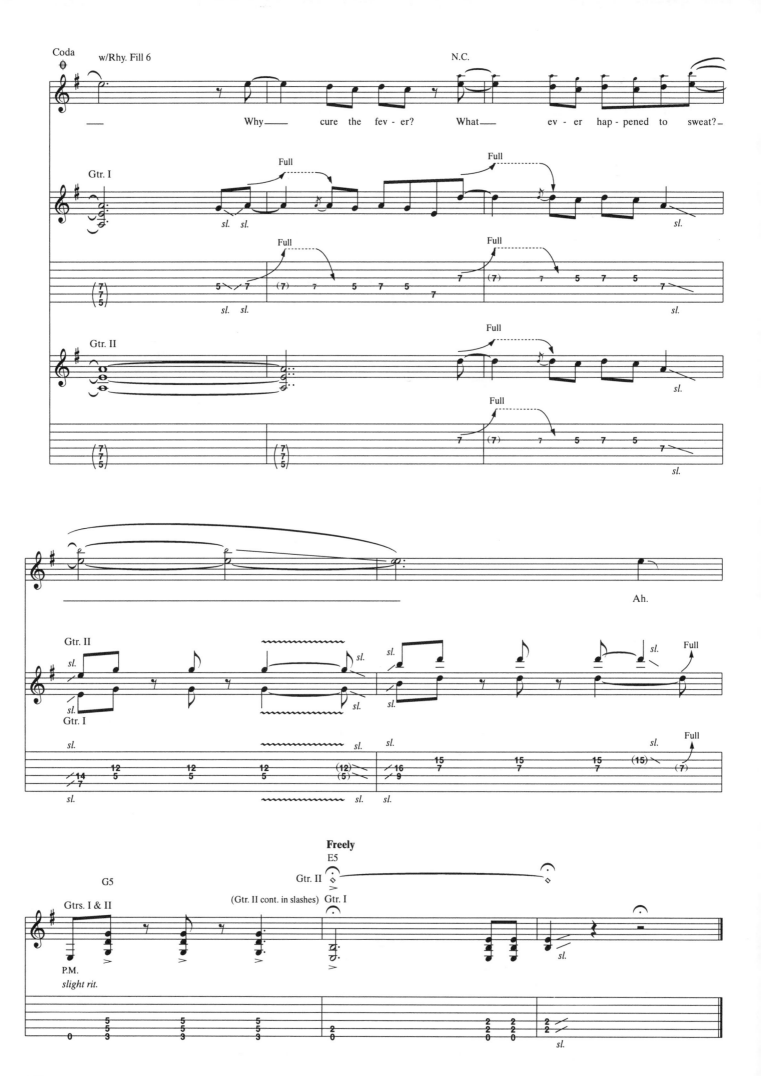

Why—— cure the fev-er? What—— ev-er hap-pened to sweat?——

Ah.

**Words and Music by James Hetfield,
Lars Ulrich and Kirk Hammett**

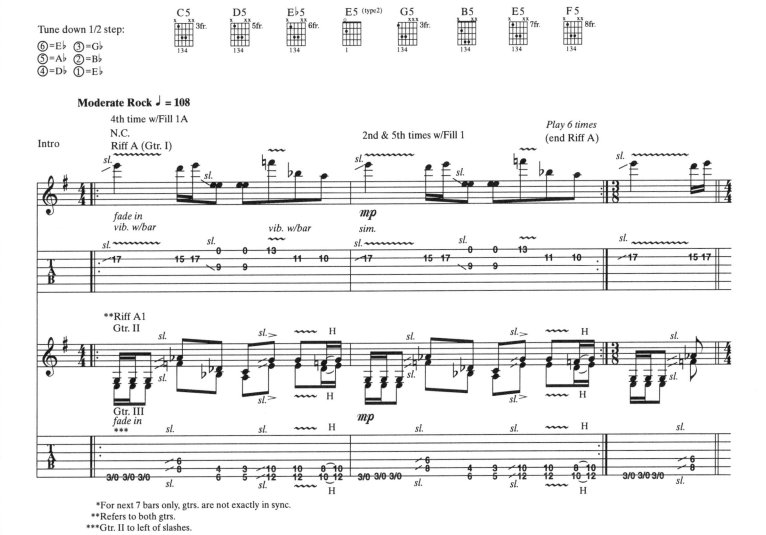

*For next 7 bars only, gtrs. are not exactly in sync.
**Refers to both gtrs.
***Gtr. II to left of slashes.

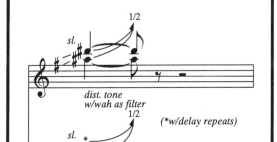

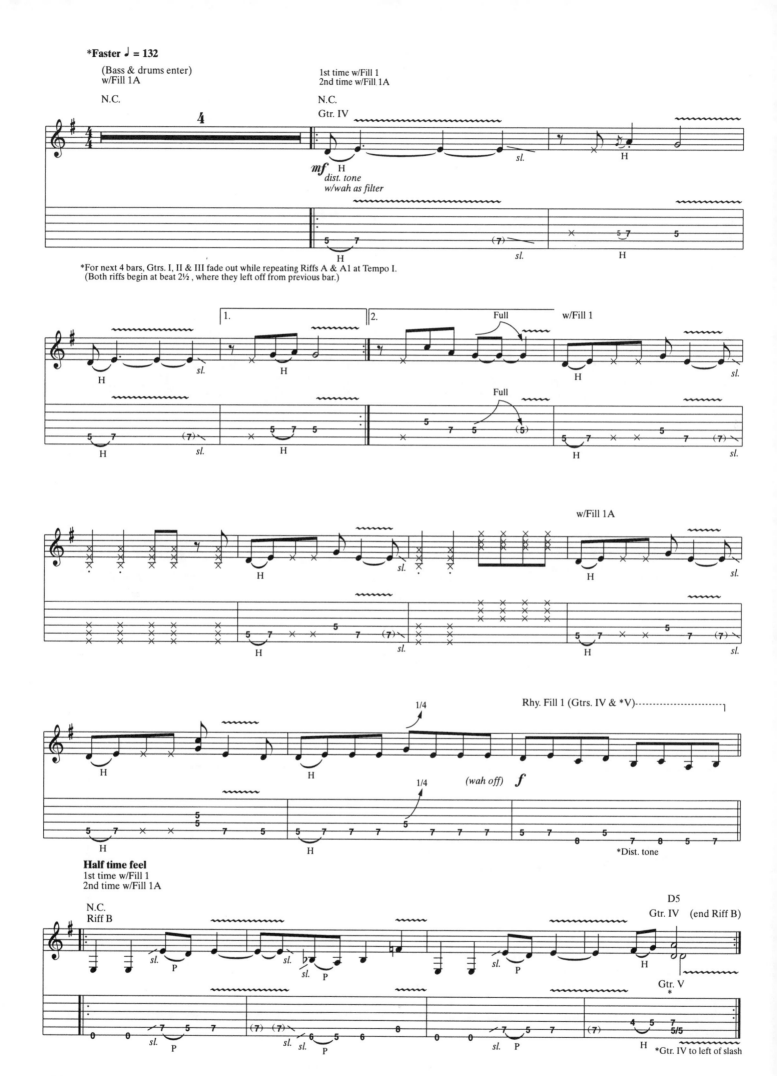

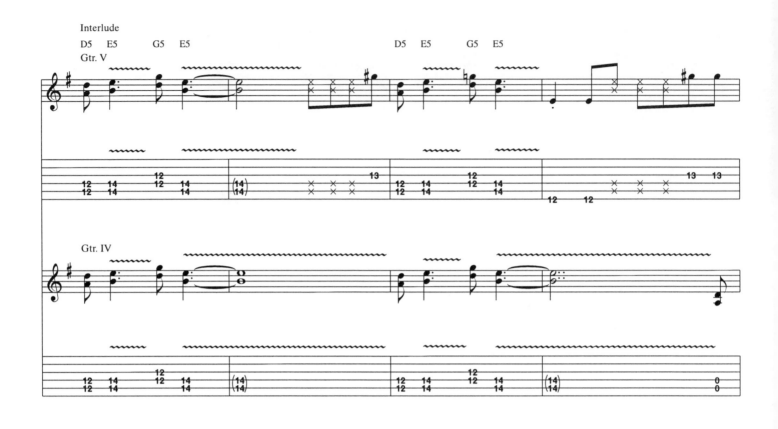

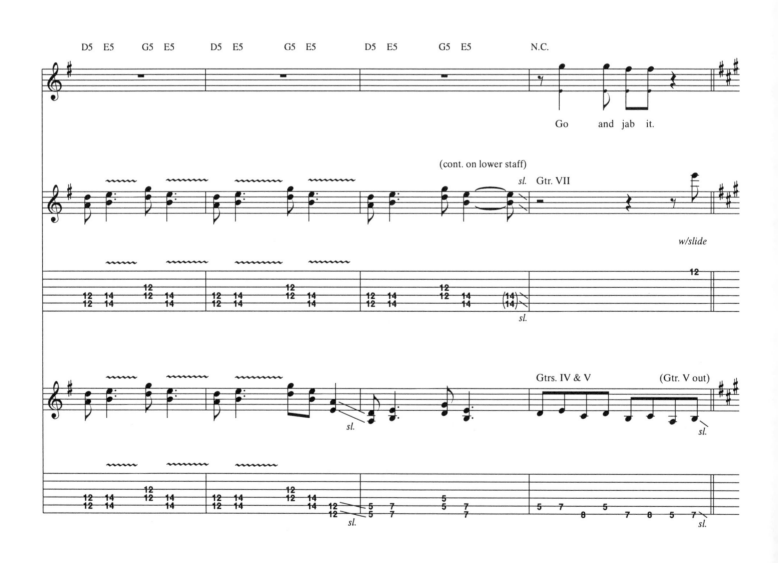

N.C.   E5

(Gtr. VII)

Gtr. IV

N.C.   E5

*w/Riff B (1¾ times) (Gtr. IV)

N.C.   D5

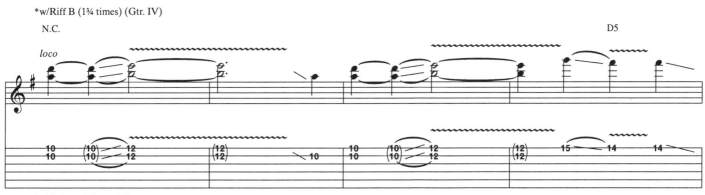

*w/slight variations ad lib

*Using a gtr. w/Les Paul–type electronics, set one vol. knob
to zero and flick toggle switch to "on" position in rhythm indicated.

*w/slight variations ad lib.

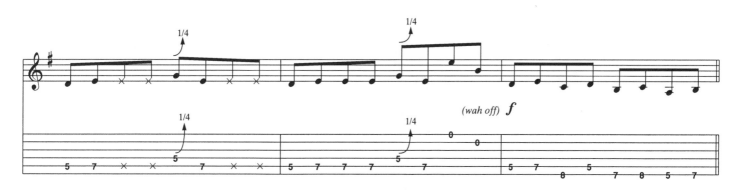

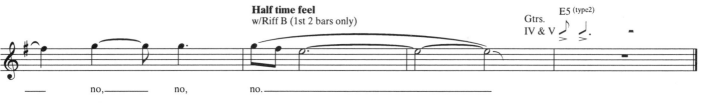

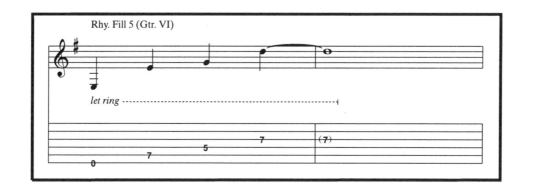

TABLATURE: A six-line staff that graphically represents the guitar fingerboard. By placing a number on the appropriate line, the string and the fret of any note can be indicated. For example:

1st string - High E	
2nd string - B	
3rd string - G	
4th string - D	
5th string - A	
6th string - Low E	

5th string, 3rd fret

2nd string, 10th fret and 3rd string, 9th fret played together

an open E chord

Definitions for Special Guitar Notation

BEND: Strike the note and bend up a half step (one fret).

BEND: Strike the note and bend up a whole step (two frets).

BEND AND RELEASE: Strike the note and bend up a half (or whole) step, then release the bend back to the original note. All three notes are tied; only the first note is struck.

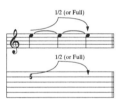

PRE-BEND: Bend the note up a half (or whole) step, then strike it.

PRE-BEND AND RELEASE: Bend the note up a half (or whole) step, strike it and release the bend back to the original note.

UNISON BEND: Strike the two notes simultaneously and bend the lower note to the pitch of the higher.

VIBRATO: Vibrate the note by rapidly bending and releasing the string with a left-hand finger.

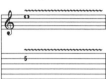

WIDE OR EXAGGERATED VIBRATO: Vibrate the pitch to a greater degree with a left-hand finger or the tremolo bar.

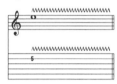

SLIDE: Strike the first note and then with the same left-hand finger move up the string to the second note. The second note is not struck.

SLIDE: Same as above, except the second note is struck.

SLIDE: Slide up to the note indicated from a few frets below.

HAMMER-ON: Strike the first (lower) note, then sound the higher note with another finger by fretting it without picking.

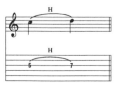

PULL-OFF: Place both fingers on the notes to be sounded. Strike the first (higher) note, then sound the lower note by pulling the finger off the higher note while keeping the lower note fretted.

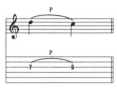

TRILL: Very rapidly alternate between the note indicated and the small note shown in parentheses by hammering on and pulling off.

TAPPING: Hammer ("tap") the fret indicated with the right-hand index or middle finger and pull off to the note fretted by the left hand.

NATURAL HARMONIC: With a left-hand finger, lightly touch the string over the fret indicated, then strike it. A chime-like sound is produced.

ARTIFICIAL HARMONIC: Fret the note normally and sound the harmonic by adding the right-hand thumb edge or index finger tip to the normal pick attack.

A.H. pitch: E

TREMOLO BAR: Drop the note by the number of steps indicated, then return to original pitch.

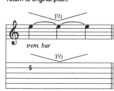

PALM MUTE: With the right hand, partially mute the note by lightly touching the string just before the bridge.

MUFFLED STRINGS: Lay the left hand across the strings without depressing them to the fretboard; strike the strings with the right hand, producing a percussive sound.

PICK SLIDE: Rub the pick edge down the length of the string to produce a scratchy sound.

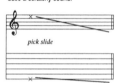

pick slide

TREMOLO PICKING: Pick the note as rapidly and continuously as possible.

trem. pick

RHYTHM SLASHES: Strum chords in rhythm indicated. Use chord voicings found in the fingering diagrams at the top of the first page of the transcription.

SINGLE-NOTE RHYTHM SLASHES: The circled number above the note name indicates which string to play. When successive notes are played on the same string, only the fret numbers are given.